AMERICAN VOICES

VIETNAMESE AMERICANS

AMERICAN VOICES

VIETNAMESE AMERICANS

by **Susan Auerbach**

Rourke Corporation, Inc.
Vero Beach, Florida 32964

Cover photo: David Fowler

∞The paper used in this book conforms to the American National Standard for Permanence of Paper for
Printed Library Materials, Z39.48-1984.

Library of Congress Cataloging-in-Publication Data
Auerbach, Susan, 1956-
    Vietnamese Americans/Susan Auerbach.
        p.   cm.—(American voices)
    Includes bibliographical references and index.
    Summary: Discusses Vietnamese who have
immigrated to the United States, their reasons for
coming, where they have settled, and how they have
contributed to their new country.
    ISBN 0-86593-136-4
    1. Vietnamese Americans—Juvenile literature. 2.
Vietnamese Americans—Biography—Juvenile
literature. [1. Vietnamese Americans.] I. Title. II.
Series.
E184.V53A94 1991   91-15806
973′.049592—dc20   CIP
                                                AC

PRINTED IN THE UNITED STATES OF AMERICA

CONTENTS

AMERICAN VOICES

VIETNAMESE AMERICANS

THE VIETNAMESE

IN NORTH AMERICA

From "Little Saigon" in Virginia to "Little Saigon" in
Southern California, Vietnamese Americans seem to be
thriving. Vietnamese stores line the neighborhood streets, and
local newspapers in Vietnamese and English advertise
community celebrations. But a few blocks from America's
largest Vietnamese shopping mall, many Vietnamese families
live in poverty.

Half of the straight-A students in a San Diego high school
are Vietnamese. But its Vietnamese students are also twice as
likely as others to drop out before graduation. What's going on
here?

The story of the Vietnamese in America is a story of both
great success and continuing struggle. It is still a new story
that is only beginning to unfold. Unlike other immigrants who
have been here for generations, the Vietnamese have been in
America for sixteen years or less. The dramatic stories of their
escape from Vietnam are better known than what has
happened to them since they arrived here. But the living
history of the Vietnamese in America is also dramatic, full of
contrasts and rapid changes.

Vietnam is an agricultural country of 62 million people in
Southeast Asia just south of China. After many years of
foreign rule, rival groups fought for control of the country
from about 1945-1975. Americans were involved in the

1

A blending of cultures: "Little Saigon," Garden Grove, California.

Vietnam War on the side of the anti-Communist South Vietnamese for twenty-five years, first as advisers and later as soldiers. Most Vietnamese who are now in America fled their homeland in the years of chaos and violence that followed the end of the war in 1975.

THE REFUGEE EXPERIENCE

There were an estimated 875,000 Vietnamese in the United States and 130,000 in Canada in 1991. The majority—more than 595,000 in the United States and 96,000 in Canada—

arrived as *refugees*, not immigrants. Immigrants *choose* to leave their native land to seek better opportunities elsewhere, often spending years making plans for permanent settlement in a new country. Refugees are *forced* to leave in fear for their lives or liberty, and often must pack their bags in a hurry. The flight of the Vietnamese was part of a general upheaval all over Southeast Asia, which also brought 350,000 war refugees from Cambodia and Laos to the United States. Most of the Vietnamese hoped they could soon return to their country.

The story of the Vietnamese in America is shaped by their refugee experience. Many suffered terrible hardships during and after the war, while escaping the country, or in primitive refugee camps while awaiting permission to enter America. Once here, they had to remake their lives from scratch and adjust to a very different culture. This was easiest for the children, who could learn English within a few months. But their parents usually had to start at the bottom of the ladder as janitors or dishwashers, even if they had held high-level jobs in Vietnam. Their strong belief in the value of education and hard work has helped many Vietnamese Americans to succeed over the years. With all that they have been through, it is no surprise that emotional problems such as depression and insomnia have been common among the refugees.

The welcome that the Vietnamese found in America was also colored by their refugee status. As refugees rather than immigrants, they were eligible for government financial help, such as welfare payments or food stamps, until they could manage on their own. Some Americans saw this aid as a national duty to refugees from a war the United States had lost. Many others, however, felt the Vietnamese had no right to be here and feared they would take away jobs from Americans. Over the years, the Vietnamese have continued to face prejudice and discrimination in some parts of the United States and Canada.

How have the Vietnamese fared in their short years in America? A lot depends on which wave of settlement brought them here: 1975, 1978-1982, or 1982 to the present. Each wave left their country and arrived here under very different conditions.

WAVES OF IMMIGRATION

The largest single group to arrive in the United States was the first wave of 125,000 Vietnamese refugees in 1975. The U.S. government set up resettlement camps to process their papers and introduce them to American life. They were matched up across the country with American sponsors (an organization, company, family, or individual) who would take responsibility for them and help them get settled. But neither the sponsors nor the refugees were prepared for their new lives together, and misunderstandings were common. Meanwhile, Canada received only a few thousand first-wave refugees, most of them sponsored by relatives already in the country.

The second wave that left Vietnam after 1978 had already lived under Communist rule after the war. After China invaded Vietnam in 1978, life was made especially hard for Vietnamese of Chinese ancestry and they were forced to leave. They became a major part of the "boat people" exodus after 1978-1979. They booked passage on ships which were often unseaworthy for a dangerous trip to nearby Asian countries. Thousands more Vietnamese escaped by night in overcrowded fishing boats. Many of these boats were attacked by pirates who came aboard to kill, rape, and rob the refugees, even pulling out their teeth for gold fillings and stealing the boats' engines. With piracy, starvation, storms, and arrests, it is thought that only half of the boat people ever reached safe shores.

The plight of the boat people attracted international attention, especially when they were turned away at Asian ports or refused rescue by other ships. Thousands were herded into unsanitary, overcrowded refugee camps in Asia, with no countries willing to take them. Eventually, both the United States and Canada made arrangements to receive large numbers of boat people. Some 269,000 Vietnamese boat people were admitted to the United States from 1979-1982. After taking in nearly 20,000 in 1979, Canada set up its first large-scale sponsorship program to admit 50,000 more Indochinese, including 25,000 Vietnamese, in 1980.

Since 1982, the number of Vietnamese refugees admitted to the United States and Canada has been drastically reduced, averaging about 23,000 and 4,000, respectively, per year. Though thousands of refugees from all over Southeast Asia still languished in Asian camps in the 1980's, the world was growing tired of hearing about their problems. New

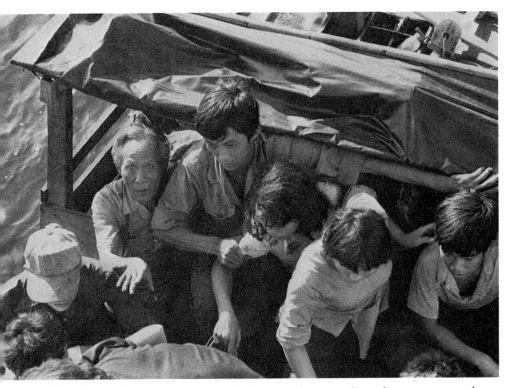

or these Vietnamese refugees, or boat people, it was a happy ending: they were rescued
fter being adrift at sea.

international laws made it harder for Vietnamese in the camps to be considered eligible for resettlement help as refugees. Meanwhile, the United States made agreements with the Vietnamese government to allow the legal departure of two types of Vietnamese directly from Vietnam: those who wished to be reunited with their families already in the United States, and Amerasians (the children of American soldiers and Vietnamese mothers) and their families.

The Vietnamese of the first two waves tended to have different social, economic, and ethnic backgrounds. For example, in the first wave, more than a quarter of the refugee heads of households had college degrees. Most were from cities and one third had worked in professional or white collar (office, technical, or managerial) jobs in Vietnam. Many spoke English due to their close ties to American military and business interests in Vietnam during the war. The second-wave refugees, on average, had far less education, job skills, and knowledge of English. For example, 38 percent had been fisherman in Vietnam compared to less than 5 percent in the first wave. The majority of second-wave refugees were from the ethnic Chinese minority in Vietnam and had run their own small family businesses there.

So far in the short story of Vietnamese in America, it is the first-wave refugees who seem to have made the most successful adjustment to American life. After early years of struggle, many found better jobs that allow them to live a middle-class life-style and send their children to college. Among them are doctors, lawyers, and engineers. Refugees from the second wave have had a harder time making ends meet, perhaps because they came from a poorer, less educated part of Vietnamese society and were demoralized by their experiences after the war. More and more Chinese Vietnamese now have their own small businesses in America, however, and with time they may be as well-off as the first wave. The

6

most recent arrivals have the advantage of coming to an America with a well-developed Vietnamese community. They may be able to find jobs among their own people without knowing English, but there are fewer government services available to them.

ETHNIC AND CULTURAL DIVERSITY

Besides the waves of settlement, other factors have made the Vietnamese Americans a diverse group. There are the ethnic Chinese who spoke Chinese and practiced many of their own customs in tightly knit communities in Vietnam, much as they do in America. There are small numbers of tribal peoples like the Montagnards and Hmong who lived with their traditional ways in the isolated mountains of Vietnam until the upheavals of war. (Most Hmong in the United States, however, are from Vietnam's neighbor country, Laos.) There are thousands of teenage Amerasians of mixed American and Vietnamese background who were never accepted in Vietnam and grew up with cruel teasing and insults. And as a new generation of 200,000 Vietnamese is born and raised in America, there are the young "Vietnamericans" who find themselves caught between two cultures.

The two main religions of Vietnamese Americans are Buddhism (an ancient Eastern religion based on meditation and seeking enlightenment) and Catholicism. More than 80 percent of the population in Vietnam was Buddhist compared to an estimated 50 percent of Vietnamese in the United States and 65 percent in Canada. Though only 10 percent of Vietnam was Catholic before the war, 40 percent of the first-wave American refugees and 28 percent of Vietnamese Canadians are Catholic. Some Vietnamese follow Chinese Confucianism or Taoism, but these do not have a formal church or clergy. There are also small Vietnamese Muslim and Protestant minorities.

7

ANCESTOR WORSHIP

Whatever their religion, most Vietnamese believe strongly in the importance of respect for their ancestors. Many still follow the traditional practice of dedicating home altars to honor relatives who have died. These altars consist of a special shelf or corner of the room where relatives' pictures are displayed along with candles, incense, religious objects, and flowers or other offerings.

On the happy occasion of *ngay gio* (anniversary of the death of an ancestor), families gather for a special meal, and food and prayers are offered in memory of ancestors. Some Vietnamese Americans, especially the elderly, travel long distances to participate in this annual event, which as many as 100 relatives may attend. They gain comfort and a strong sense of family unity from this symbolic connection to those who came before them. By fulfilling their duty to their ancestors, the Vietnamese believe that they are insuring the well-being of present and future generations.

Ancestors are also remembered with food, ceremonies, and blessings on Tet, the Vietnamese New Year. This celebration usually falls in early February, as does Chinese New Year, according to the changing dates of the lunar (moon-based) calendar. The most important Vietnamese holiday, Tet is celebrated in America with midnight firecrackers, drums, and green *banh chu'ng* rice cakes. Children are given "lucky money" in red envelopes by their families and the many friends and business associates who come to visit. The days before Tet are seen as a good time to clean the house, shop for new clothes and gifts, pay off debts, and settle disagreements. It is believed that whatever happens on Tet will affect one's good luck for the coming year.

FAMILY VALUES

Vietnamese Americans share other basic values and

Even in America, the extended family is still a vital part of the Vietnamese culture. Pictured here is the Chuy family living in Ohio.

traditions which make them distinct in America. The family rather than the individual is considered the center of a person's life, and family interest comes first before self-interest. It was common in Vietnam to live together in extended families of three generations or more (grandparents, parents, children, and so forth). This tradition has been hard to maintain in America, but most Vietnamese households are still large by American standards. In 1980, the Thoa Nguyen family of nine was reunited in Michigan after six failed attempts to escape from

Vietnam as well as two years of being scattered in prisons and refugee camps. The parents, who had been a schoolteacher and principal in Vietnam, worked picking fruit for several years in order to send their children to college. They told *Readers Digest* that their family's survival and success was due to their intense loyalty to the family above all else.

Children are expected to be obedient, as in the Vietnamese proverb, "Children sit where their parents place them." Young people are supposed to show respect for their elders, for example, waiting for the oldest person to sit down before eating dinner and serving them during the meal. In Vietnam, parents usually picked wives for their sons. Like many customs of Vietnamese family life, this practice has broken down in America. Increasing numbers of Vietnamese youth are taking up dating, American style, to the great dismay of their parents. There is even a nationwide Vietnamese computer dating service based in California.

Changes in family life are one of the greatest tensions in the Vietnamese American community today. In traditional Vietnam, most women had very little education and were expected to be homemakers who obeyed their parents, husbands, and older sons. During the war, many women were forced to take jobs to support their families. This situation has continued in America, tipping the old balance of power between wives and their husbands, who often have trouble finding good jobs themselves. The Vietnamese-American divorce rate and the number of households headed by one parent are on the rise. The elderly generally speak no English and cannot drive; they complain of feeling isolated, afraid, and too dependent on their children. Parents often feel cut off by their children, who do not obey them here as they would have in Vietnam. Teenagers who prefer hamburgers to egg rolls and seem to blend easily into American society struggle with the strict rules set by their parents. The stress of getting settled in

10

America has thus divided both the sexes and the generations among the Vietnamese.

SUCCESS AND SORROW

As they continue to arrive in America, the Vietnamese form an ever larger part of the fast-growing Asian-American population of seven million. Vietnamese are now the third largest Asian-American group after Filipinos and Chinese. Asian Americans have often been called a "model minority"

Anh Tuan Nguyen-Huynh, of Ohio, came to the United States from Vietnam in 1981. Five years later, he is a scholarship winner in Westinghouse's national Science Talent Search competition.

for their achievements in the academic and professional worlds. The Vietnamese who have been here so short a time seem to many to be an especially remarkable minority, with their science scholarship students, successful professionals, and active businesses. "Perhaps never before in American history have so many refugees succeeded economically so fast and so well," writes anthropologist James Freeman in a recent study.

Westinghouse Electric Corporation

Another example of a science scholarship student and finalist in the 1986 Westinghouse Science Talent Search is Hong B. Huynh of California.

But, he adds, "beneath the surface of success in America lies sorrow." Many Vietnamese Americans Freeman interviewed told him they do not feel "at ease" in their new lives. "Here in America, we have all the material comforts," said one businessman. "But the joy and sentiment are not like we had in Vietnam. There when we went out from the home, we laughed, we jumped. . . . Here, I only know what goes on in my home; my neighbor knows only what goes on in his home." Some Vietnamese still dream of returning to their country, as in this excerpt from a poem by a young man who came to America alone at the age of sixteen:

> I don't know whether my homeland is still existing.
> With grief, I see months and days passing.
> I miss you, O Vietnam, where repose generations of my
>   ancestors.
> I miss my small village stretching out amidst the ocean.
> Where is my family now? I wonder . . .

What will it take for the Vietnamese to feel at home in America? Over the years, they have left cold climates and small towns for cities in California and Texas. Together with those who speak their language and share their values, they have formed large communities. They have set up organizations to preserve their culture and to help the latest arrivals. Like other ethnic groups, the Vietnamese are making choices about what to accept and what to reject in American culture. They are moving from an uprooted refugee phase to a more settled phase as they put down roots in America and strengthen their own community. With its unique accomplishments and troubles, their unfinished story continues to unfold.

THE COMMUNITY

A typical weekend in Southern California's "Little Saigon" finds Vietnamese families doing many of the same things as their American neighbors, though the details are different. They crowd the local shopping mall, where their purchases might include perfume to send to relatives in Vietnam or a traditional woman's *ao dai* outfit (long-sleeved, high-necked, knee-length tunic with side slits over narrow pants) to wear to a wedding. They stock up on Vietnamese and French-style sweets at the bakery, or they eat a fast food lunch of *pho* (hearty beef rice noodle soup). Some worship at one of the area's Vietnamese Catholic churches or Buddhist temples. Others relax by playing a game of soccer, pool, or *co tuong* (a Chinese form of chess), by reading one of the two dozen local Vietnamese newspapers, by tuning in to "Freedom Television" in Vietnamese, or by visiting friends or family. Children might study Vietnamese in a community Saturday school, play *nhay day* (Chinese jump rope), do homework, or help out in the family grocery store.

As the hub of the "refugees' capital" of Orange County, Little Saigon is probably livelier than most places where Vietnamese live. But from Queens, New York, to San Jose, California, and from Houston, Texas, to Montreal, Canada, the Vietnamese have been quick to build their own communities in North America. Like other immigrants, they have established organizations, religious institutions, media, and businesses to meet their special needs. They have also tried to maintain certain Vietnamese customs and values in the home,

14

Leisure time is spent in many ways; here Vietnamese American students get serious about volleyball.

sometimes bringing them into conflict with the rest of American society.

COMMUNITY ORGANIZATIONS

As early as 1976, when there were still only a few thousand Vietnamese in all of Canada, the Toronto Vietnamese Fraternal Association sponsored a cultural evening of song and poetry in honor of Tet. In 1985, 30,000 Vietnamese Americans went to Camp Pendleton in Southern California for a tenth year reunion of their refugee camp days (see pages 41 and 43). In the years between and since, several hundred Vietnamese organizations have been formed in the United States and many occasions celebrated; the Vietnamese Canadian Federation coordinates the activities of nineteen organizations across Canada.

Most Vietnamese organizations are local groups that get together for fun and socializing. They organize holiday events such as outdoor Tet carnivals with game booths, food, and fireworks, or variety shows in rented halls featuring famous Vietnamese pop singers. In the Uptown district of Chicago, children stage an evening parade for the Mid-Autumn Festival with paper lanterns and dragon dances done to drums and cymbals. Some social groups such as Vietnamese Lions clubs and scout troops are modeled on American organizations. Others respond to Vietnamese concerns such as reverence for ancestors by buying up block of cemetery plots for their members, as in California's Santa Clara County.

Groups also form for educational and cultural purposes, especially to pass on traditions to children. For example, the Huong Viet School was established in East Oakland, California, in 1987 to teach the Vietnamese language to children ages 5 to 16. Every Saturday, its 200 students learn not only written Vietnamese but also their native music, history, and customs, such as respect for parents. Other cultural

16

e Tet celebration, or the Vietnamese New Year's celebration, is always a major event, thering the entire community together for good times.

organizations stress Vietnamese dance or martial arts training, sharing their culture with Americans in performances at festivals and fairs. The Vietnamese Canadian Federation runs a community resource center and library in Ottawa, in addition to its many Vietnamese language and heritage classes.

Other groups serve college students, women, youth, and ethnic minorities (for example, the Vietnamese Minorities of the Nong Folks Mutual Association in Los Angeles). The Chinese Vietnamese typically form their own Indochina

Chinese organizations. There are also professional associations of lawyers, engineers, fishermen, and so forth. Small political groups have sprung up around former leaders from Vietnam living in the United States; their purposes range from condemning the current regime in Vietnam to encouraging the United States to normalize diplomatic relations with Hanoi.

In a common immigrant pattern, the Vietnamese have banded together for mutual aid in getting settled in America. The Vietnamese American Association in Oklahoma City in 1977 was one of the first to get government funds to sponsor its own English classes, job referral program, and the training of Vietnamese mental health counselors. Today, Vietnamese resettlement organizations are usually staffed by Vietnamese professionals, which makes them more comfortable and welcoming to their Vietnamese clients. One large and active example is the Vietnamese Community of Orange County, Inc., which offers free meals to the elderly, a youth crime prevention program, job training for adults, translation and help with immigration paperwork, and other services. Other groups combine social services and activities (housing referrals and volleyball games at the Boulder, Colorado, Vietnamese Alliance; youth counseling and the sponsorship of a community garden at the Vietnamese Mutual Assistance Association of East Dallas, Texas). As government services decrease, Vietnamese-American leaders are promoting the need for self-help. A number of private foundations have recently been formed by wealthier Vietnamese to support scholarships and special projects.

RELIGIOUS LIFE

By far the biggest and richest group of Vietnamese organizations in America are religious. The many Catholics in the first wave of refugees started their own Vietnamese churches, sometimes reuniting parishes around their original

priest from Vietnam. Of the estimated 100 Vietnamese
Catholic communities in the United States today, the largest of
twenty-two official parishes is New Orleans (10,000
parishioners), followed by Port Arthur-Beaumont and Houston,
Texas. Recently, smaller numbers of Vietnamese have become
involved in Protestant movements, as in the Vietnamese
Church of the Full Gospel in Long Beach, California.

The Buddhist religion practiced by half the Vietnamese-
American population is less familiar to Americans. Among
their central beliefs is the idea that people have past lives, and
that these affect how they live in present and future lives.
Their religion stresses detachment from the material world and
the practice of meditation on an eight-part path to
enlightenment.

The eighty Vietnamese Buddhist temples in America are

The Catholic Church plays an important role in the Vietnamese American community.

more than just places of worship. They are community centers where Vietnamese find reminders of the comforts of home and the feeling of a big extended family. Some temples have been active in sponsoring, sheltering, and resettling refugees.

The oldest temple in America, Chua Viet Nam in Los Angeles, was founded in 1976. It houses about twenty monks who act as spiritual advisers and lead chanting to drums and bells at specified hours each day. Whereas in Vietnam, monks were supported by the community, in the United States they often get regular jobs outside the temple to support themselves. Every Sunday, the community offers them money and a ceremonial meal. As women prepare traditional vegetarian dishes, children play in the courtyard or take part in meetings of the Long Hoa Vietnamese Buddhist Youth Group. Worshippers remove their shoes and enter the shrine room to pray, meditate, and chant in front of gold statues of Buddha, "the Enlightened One" who founded their religion. Though not officially a Buddhist practice, some temple visitors consult fortune sticks, each of which has a Chinese character on it that corresponds to a poem in Vietnamese with advice for the person's situation. For Buddha's Birthday in May, the temple is decorated with flowers and flags, dignitaries speak, and there may be a parade with floats, brass bands, and dragon dancers.

Both temples and churches in the Vietnamese community observe the Tet holiday with special services and celebrations. They also attend to the needs of Vietnamese marking periods of mourning or the anniversaries of their ancestors' deaths. Many Vietnamese consult fortune tellers or astrologers, whatever their religion. This is especially important before building a home, choosing a gravesite, or setting a wedding date to make sure that everything is in alignment with the earth's forces for good luck.

MEDIA AND LANGUAGE

Besides organizations and religion, Vietnamese in America maintain their ties to one another in more informal ways. As in Vietnam, they gather with friends in *pho* soup shops, teahouses, cafés, poolhalls, and even at nightclubs with Vietnamese entertainment. They meet and exchange news at Vietnamese businesses, many of which have a community bulletin board or sell Vietnamese-American newspapers. These, plus Vietnamese-language radio programs, keep the community members informed not only of their growing population and culture in America but also of the latest developments in Vietnam and in American immigration policy. Vietnamese Canadians read a dozen thick Vietnamese magazines as well as many local organization newsletters. These Vietnamese media, along with a small number of Vietnamese book publishers and libraries, help keep both language and culture alive in America.

Vietnamese is still spoken in the vast majority of Vietnamese-American households. But it is less and less used by the young people, especially those born here. As one high school student wrote, "I hated it when Americans teased me about my language. Maybe that's why I don't talk in Vietnamese in front of Americans anymore. I think, dream, and pray in English. I can still read Vietnamese, but very slowly." On the other hand, older Vietnamese often have trouble mastering the long words and changing verb tenses of English.

In Vietnam, people give their family name first followed by their first and middle names (for example, Nguyen Thanh Xuan or with an English name, Smith John William). In America, many Vietnamese put the family name last to avoid confusion (for example, Thanh Xuan Nguyen). There are only about 30 Vietnamese family names, with Nguyen (pronounced win) by far the most common. Other typical last names include Ky, Le, Lee, Pham, Tran, Trinh, and Vu. When Vietnamese people need help in a strange American city, or a real estate agent is looking for Vietnamese customers, they may simply look up some of these names in the local phone book to find their compatriots.

SOCIAL CUSTOMS

Besides language, food and other customs make the daily life of Vietnamese Americans distinct. Meals generally include *nuoc mam*, a fermented fish sauce with a strong odor that is a staple of the diet in Vietnam. Families working long hours may no longer have the time to make elaborate traditional foods, which are a combination of Chinese and French influences. Large communities have restaurants and bakeries to supply specialties like the delicate *cha-gio* (an eggroll of crab, noodles, dried mushrooms, and other ingredients wrapped in rice paper) or the sticky, sesame seed-covered *banh cam* dessert.

Vietnamese health practices are influenced by traditions of Eastern, rather than Western, medicine. Some Vietnamese Americans prefer to see an Asian specialist in acupuncture or herbal remedies, rather than seek help from American doctors, who favor using hospitals and prescription drugs. A traditional treatment for fever and illness is tiger balm ointment rubbed into the skin with the edge of a rough coin. This custom of *cao gio*, which can leave red marks on the skin, has sometimes been condemned as child abuse by American school and health officials.

Another Vietnamese custom which seems to clash with American ways and laws concerns discipline for children. According to a Vietnamese proverb, "When we love our children, we give them a beating; when we hate our children, we give them sweet words." This goes along with the value placed on people being modest, rather than boasting or competitive, and children obeying their parents, who make great sacrifices for them. Beating one's child is meant to show concern, rather than abuse. Refugee organizations have tried to educate the Vietnamese about American child protection laws and school rules, while making Americans more aware of Vietnamese customs and values.

The social habits of Vietnamese also contrast with those of many Americans. Due to their Confucian heritage, Vietnamese tend to be more formal and reserved in their style of relating to other people. They do not consider it polite to look someone straight in the eye or to disagree with them openly. They often smile or say "yes," when actually they are upset, so they will not hurt the other person's feelings. This behavior led to many misunderstandings between American sponsors and first-wave Vietnamese refugees in making arrangements for suitable housing and jobs. Likewise, Vietnamese students who have been taught to be extremely respectful of teachers may at first be uncomfortable with the debates, personal essays, and general informality of American schools. Of course, the young generation tends to be less tied to traditional ways and more adaptable to the freedom of American life-styles.

COMMUNITY TENSIONS

As Vietnamese-American communities become better established, they face not only conflicts with their adopted culture but problems within their own community. The top concerns cited in a 1989 *Los Angeles Times* poll of Vietnamese Americans were gangs and crime. Vietnamese gang members tend to be teenage boys who came to the United States alone, speak little English, and do poorly in school. They prey on Vietnamese businesses and homes in some American cities. Though they represent only a tiny percentage of Vietnamese youth, they receive a lot of attention in the press, creating a stereotype of the community that most Vietnamese think is unfair.

Another key problem often mentioned by Vietnamese community leaders is mental health. In Vietnam, there were no psychologists or counselors to help with emotional problems; families took care of their own. In America, many refugees suffer from post-traumatic stress disorder—a delayed reaction to all the troubles they have seen during wartime and in leaving their country. Almost twice as many Vietnamese as Americans (49 percent versus 26 percent) described themselves as feeling depressed, hopeless, or worthless in a 1984 mental health survey. Vietnamese community professionals and religious leaders try to advise these people in ways that respect their culture.

There is also reportedly tension between the better-educated, wealthier first-wave Vietnamese refugees and those who came later, having suffered under Communism and in dangerous escapes (see chapters 1 and 4). The earlier settlers often see the newcomers as being unwilling to work hard and too dependent on welfare, while the newcomers resent the established people for their privilege and for looking down on them. The leaders of Vietnamese community organizations in both the United States and Canada tend to be from the first wave; their better command of English makes them better able to act as bridges to American society.

Whatever their wave of settlement, all Vietnamese Americans share tremendous concern for and guilt about relatives left behind in Vietnam. They send them money and precious American products such as vitamins, medicines, cosmetics, and fabrics in frequent care packages. Even those on low incomes try to sponsor their relatives to join them in their own cramped homes in America. Increasingly in recent years, Vietnamese Americans are travelling home to visit family in Vietnam, especially for the Tet holiday. No matter what safety, comforts, and opportunities they may have found in America, they have not forgotten the loved ones and the tombs of their ancestors which remain in their native country.

VIETNAM

Many things have changed in their native land since the first wave of Vietnamese Americans left. The devastation of thirty years of war can still be seen in damaged buildings, leftover bomb shells, and parts of the countryside made barren by chemicals used by American troops. Saigon, once known for its elegant tree-lined streets and European atmosphere, is now a smaller, shabbier Ho Chi Minh City. The Vietnamese Communist Party rules as the only political party and depends heavily on foreign aid from the Soviet Union. Vietnam today is one of the world's poorest countries, with its 62 million citizens earning an average of $500 a year.

Some things have remained the same, however. Vietnam is still primarily an agricultural country, one of the world's five top rice producers. Daily life for the 80 percent of the people who live in Vietnam's 16,000 villages has not changed much: Farmers still work long hours cultivating their rice paddies and other crops using wooden plows pulled by water buffalo. Rice is still the most important part of the Vietnamese diet, along with fish, fruits, and vegetables.

Culturally, the majority of Vietnamese are still Buddhist; there are also four million Vietnamese Catholics, a small number of Muslims in the south, and members of several other sects including Protestants. Most Vietnamese have altars to their ancestors in their homes and take part in the three-day Tet celebration. Whatever their level of education, they show a great love of poetry. Many write their own verse and memorize classics like "The Tale of Kieu," a poem of 3,254 lines about a girl's heroic struggle to preserve her family's honor. Musical comedy remains popular, as does Chinese-style opera with its extravagant costumes and tales of warriors, demons, and princesses. Vietnamese artisans continue to make traditional woodblock prints and shiny lacquerware. The government allows a small film industry but looks down on other modern arts, such as painting and rock music.

The people of today's Vietnam, like the refugees who left, share a deep pride in Vietnam's ancient civilization. Few Americans know much about this land that is 9,000 miles away, and even less about the history and culture that the Vietnamese brought with them to America.

LAND AND PEOPLE

Vietnam is located in Southeast Asia on the Indochina peninsula—so-called because it lies between India to the west and China to the northeast. Its neighbors are China to the north, Laos and Kampuchea (formerly Cambodia) to the west, and the South China Sea (part of the Pacific Ocean) to the east. It is a long, narrow, S-shaped country of 127,000 square miles, about the size of the state of New Mexico. It has sometimes been called the "small dragon" because of its shape, and its close physical and cultural ties with China (the "big dragon"). It has also been compared to a long bamboo pole with a rice basket at each end. Both the Red River Delta in the north and the larger Mekong Delta in the south are fertile, low-lying areas famous for their rice cultivation. Running between them from north to south are the Annamite Mountains and the narrow sea coast. Vietnam has a tropical climate with hot, wet summers and cool, dry winters. The rainy season, which can last from May to October, is marked by heavy monsoon rains which come at predictable times each day.

About 90 percent of the people living in Vietnam are ethnic

Vietnamese. They were descended from a combination of Thai, Chinese, and Indonesian peoples who made up the earliest tribes living in the area. The Vietnamese language reflects this history. It is thought to be of Indonesian origin, but includes many Chinese words and was originally written in Chinese-style characters. In the 1600's, European missionaries developed Quoc Ngu, a system of writing Vietnamese with the Roman alphabet (the same one used in English), which was not fully accepted in Vietnam until the 1900's. Written Vietnamese has markings above and below the letters for accents and six tones (for example, with the voice rising or falling in pitch) which affect a word's meaning. Non-Vietnamese ethnic groups in the country, such as the mountain tribes, Cambodians, Thai, and Chinese, also speak their own languages.

EARLY HISTORY: CHINESE INFLUENCE

Vietnamese history can be understood according to four main periods: 1,000 years of Chinese rule, 900 years of independence, 100 years of French colonial rule (though only 62 years as an official colony), and the post-1945 period (see Time Line). According to an old legend, the country began when a Chinese warlord and an emperor's daughter gave birth to 100 eggs which hatched 100 sons, taking 50 of them to the north and 50 to the south to rule the land. Divisions between north and south have been part of Vietnam's troubled history ever since.

The first known organized state in Vietnam was the kingdom of Nam Viet in the north in 208 B.C. It was conquered by the Chinese in 111 B.C. and named Annam (Pacified South), the southernmost part of the Chinese empire. For more than 1,000 years, the Chinese had a tremendous influence on Vietnamese life, especially in government, literature, and philosophy. They introduced Confucianism, a system of beliefs that stressed the importance of obeying authority based on education and ethics. Through exams, people could become mandarins, or government officials, based on their knowledge and merit as individuals rather than their birth.

The Vietnamese continued to speak their own language and resented attempts by the Chinese to interfere in local affairs. They were also burdened with heavy taxes and forced labor or army service to support the vast Chinese empire. There were many rebellions, like that led by the Trung sisters in A.D. 39; they ruled as queens for a few years, then drowned themselves in sorrow upon defeat.

Chinese rule collapsed in A.D. 939 when the empire became too weak to control all its territories. There followed 900 years of independence under eight long Vietnamese dynasties or ruling families. These emperors made Buddhism the official religion, set up new educational and legal systems, and built bridges and roads as well as magnificent pagodas and tombs in the imperial city of Hue.

Wars were frequent in this period. The Chinese ruled again briefly from 1407-1427 until they were finally subdued by the hero Le Loi, a fisherman turned soldier. He set up the capital in Hanoi and led the country into a flourishing time under the Le dynasty. Vietnam expanded to the south in 1471 by defeating the kingdom of Champa, which controlled parts of what is now central and southern coastal Vietnam. Between 1620 and 1674, two rival landlord families, the Trinh in the north and the Nguyen in the south, fought constantly for territory. After 100 years of peace, the Tayson rebellion again plunged the country into war. Finally, in 1802, Nguyen Anh unified the north and the south, named the country Vietnam, and began the Nguyen dynasty, which lasted until 1945.

THE FRENCH COLONIAL PERIOD

Meanwhile, Westerners had become interested in Vietnam. Portuguese, Dutch, and English traders began arriving in the 1500's. They were followed in the 1600's by French missionaries, who aimed to spread the Catholic religion. At various times, the suspicious Vietnamese emperors had the Catholics killed, imprisoned, or expelled from the country. But more kept arriving, paving the way for French political influence.

In the 1800's, the French were looking for ways to expand their power in Asia, especially in trade with China. They began to have a major presence in Vietnam in the 1850's. By 1883, they had unified the areas of Tonkin, Annam, and Cochin-China and declared Vietnam an official colony of France. They also took over neighboring Laos and Cambodia, which together with Vietnam became known as French Indochina.

The French saw themselves as a superior people bringing civilization to a backward country. They closed 20,000 Vietnamese schools during their rule and set up their own schools, imposing Catholicism, the French language, and Quoc Ngu (Vietnamese written in the Roman alphabet). They encouraged and favored the settlement of Chinese merchants in Vietnam because of their business contacts with China. The French also started large rubber plantations and increased rice production. But their rule was harsh for the Vietnamese peasants, many of whom lost their land, paid steep taxes, and went hungry.

HO CHI MINH AND RESISTANCE TO FRENCH RULE

After 900 years of independence and their own culture, the Vietnamese were not content under foreign rule. Secret societies were formed to resist the French. Members of these societies were inspired by nationalism: the belief that the people of a country have a right to rule themselves and determine their own future. The best organized group was the League for the Independence of Vietnam or Viet Minh, founded in 1941 by Ho Chi Minh.

Ho Chi Minh is so important to modern Vietnam that he has been called its George Washington. Born in 1890 to a nationalist family, he went to the best French schools in Hue. During thirty-five years of exile, he lived in France, the Soviet Union, and China, while also visiting the United States and much of Asia. He learned about different kinds of government and agitated for the independence of his country through his writings and meetings with European leaders. He returned to Vietnam in 1941 to recruit members of the Viet Minh movement. Though a small, delicate man who looked like a scholar, Ho became a powerful leader who attracted people from all walks of life to his nationalist cause and Communist beliefs.

The events of 1945 in Vietnam were momentous for the country's future. The Japanese briefly occupied the country near the end of World War II. Their control of the rice supply set off a famine in which two million Vietnamese died of starvation. After the Japanese surrendered, Ho Chi Minh declared Vietnam independent in September. But the French were determined to regain their control over Indochina. Thus began the First Indochina War of 1946-1954 between the French and the Viet Minh.

THE FIRST INDOCHINA WAR

Known in France as "the dirty war," these eight years of fighting set the tone for what was to happen later when America became directly involved. The dedicated Viet Minh under General Vo Nguyen Giap waged guerrilla war (with surprise attacks and ambushes in many isolated areas) rather than conventional war (where the enemy is fought on one

32

front). With the help of arms supplied by China, they controlled much of southern Vietnam. The United States paid for two thirds of the French war effort beginning in 1950, obligated by the Truman Doctrine to help peoples who were fighting Communist movements. But the conventional war tactics of the French did not work well in Vietnam. They were defeated at the battle of Dien Bien Phu in 1954. Though they lost the war, the French left their mark on Vietnam in its political system, grand style of architecture, schools and hospitals, the Paris-like atmosphere of cities like Saigon—and even Vietnamese cuisine.

The international Geneva Accords that ended the war set a central boundary between north and south Vietnam at the seventeenth parallel latitude. The north was to be ruled by the Communists and the south by anti-Communist nationalists. About a million people left the north for the south, prompted by the Viet Minh's taking over of land and killing landlords. Most of those who went south were Catholics, Chinese Vietnamese, or others who feared punishment for their anti-Communist beliefs. Many of these 1954 refugees would later leave Vietnam for America as second-time refugees in 1975.

THE VIETNAM WAR

Soon after Vietnam was divided, the North Vietnamese based in Hanoi began planning for continued war to unify it. This would become known as the Second Indochina War or Vietnam War. The North Vietnamese organized the Viet Cong to fight for the Communist cause in the south. They were opposed by the ARVN (Army of the Republic of Vietnam) in South Vietnam, which received aid and training from the Americans. Beginning in the late 1950's, both sides killed thousands of enemy officials and leaders, as well as innocent people, in a war of terrorism.

Ngo Dinh Diem became president of the new Republic of

United States and South Vietnamese soldiers work together in a rescue operation 16, 1964) during the Vietnam War.

Vietnam in the south in 1955. The United States supported the anti-Communist Diem in the belief that if Vietnam fell to the Communists, they would soon take over other parts of Asia. But Diem was never a popular leader with his own people, and his government became known for corruption and ineffectiveness. When Vietnamese Buddhists protested Diem's policies, thousands were imprisoned and their activities restricted. In 1963, the world was shocked by photos of a

Buddhist monk who set himself on fire in a protest suicide. That same year, the government was toppled in a coup and Diem assassinated.

AMERICAN PARTICIPATION IN THE WAR

The history of the controversial Vietnam War is still being written. From America's point of view, it was "the longest war," about twenty-five years of involvement that led to sharp political divisions and change in American society. For the Vietnamese, it was a continuation of the struggle for the country's future which had begun years earlier against the French. Almost 58,000 American soldiers died in this war, compared to 1,300,000 Vietnamese (including 363,000 civilians). Most of what we know about the war through books and movies in America is seen through the eyes of Americans, rather than Vietnamese—a point which embitters many Vietnamese Americans.

By 1962, the Americans had 12,000 military advisers in Vietnam. The first combat troops were sent in 1965 and began heavy bombing of North Vietnam which lasted until 1968. By then, 500,000 American soldiers and the South Vietnamese army were having trouble fighting the Viet Cong in jungle and village areas. Though poorly armed, the Viet Cong used booby traps and nighttime hit-and-run attacks, as well as hidden tunnels containing hospitals, sleeping quarters, and storage areas for food and weapons. They also had the support of many villagers, either through force (opponents were killed as examples) or through the appeal of Communism as a system that might liberate Vietnam from foreigners. A quarter of the rural South Vietnamese population fled their villages because of the fighting, crowding into miserable shack cities on the edges of Saigon, Hue, and Danang.

In January, 1968, the Communists attacked more than 100 cities and bases in South Vietnam in the massive Tet

Offensive. This event is considered a turning point in the war for three reasons. First, the Viet Cong were tremendously weakened when the battles were over. Second, American public opinion began to turn against the war in reaction to the high casualties. Third, as a result of these changes, peace negotiations were started in Paris that May.

ENDING THE WAR

Negotiations continued off and on for several years. The North Vietnamese would not compromise until American troops left Vietnam. America wanted "peace with honor" while South Vietnamese President Nguyen Van Thieu feared that his government would be left in the lurch. Each side kept on fighting, with the United States extending the war with secret bombing of Cambodia and Laos in 1969-1970. This sparked the largest antiwar protests to date in the United States and increasing pressure from Congress to get America out of Vietnam. A peace agreement was finally signed in Paris and all American troops were removed in 1973.

The war was technically over for the United States, though many advisers stayed on. However, the fighting was far from over for the Vietnamese. The North Vietnamese army was a well-trained force of 500,000 by 1974, bolstered by aid from the Soviet Union and China. The South Vietnamese army, which had depended heavily on American troops and money, felt abandoned by the troop withdrawals and drastic cuts in American aid. The North Vietnamese began their final push to take over the south in January of 1975. When they reached the central highlands in March, thousands of South Vietnamese soldiers deserted and joined more than 400,000 civilians fleeing south to the coast in panic. By April 29, 1975, the North Vietnamese had reached Saigon and the Communists declared victory on April 30.

On the same two days, the first major groups of Vietnamese

refugees to be resettled in America left Vietnam by American helicopters and ships. Over the next fifteen years, an estimated one million Vietnamese left their country. The American connection that more than half of them eventually made was a direct result of the Vietnam War and its aftermath.

WHY AMERICA?

The sudden end to the Vietnam War in 1975 left both the South Vietnamese and the Americans unprepared. No one knew at the time how closely linked the fates of hundreds of thousands of Vietnamese were soon to be to the United States and, later, Canada.

Why should so many Vietnamese refugees have ended up in America rather than someplace else? First, close ties from the war years made many Americans feel obliged to help their South Vietnamese business and military associates, employees, friends, spouses, and children. For example, 8,000 workers for American corporations in Vietnam were brought directly to the United States and given jobs by their old employers, such as Chase Manhattan Bank. Secondly, the U.S. government had a tradition of taking in refugees fleeing from Communist revolutions, such as Hungarians in the 1950's and Cubans in the 1960's. There were also compelling humanitarian reasons to welcome the later wave of boat people. Finally, as more Vietnamese became settled in the United States and Canada, they made arrangements for the immigration of their relatives still in Vietnam.

REASONS FOR LEAVING: THE FIRST WAVE

As in any mass movement of peoples, there were specific "push factors"—conditions that made people desperate to leave Vietnam—and "pull factors"—conditions that drew them to America. These were different for each of the three waves of Vietnamese who came to America from 1975 to the present.

The push factors that operated in April, 1975, as the Communists closed in on Saigon are easy to determine. South Vietnamese government and military leaders, as well as those who had worked for the Americans, feared that they would be put in prison or executed. Other groups, such as wealthy businessmen, Buddhists, and Catholics who had migrated from the north in 1954, worried that they would not be able to live freely under Communist rule. Thousands of other Vietnamese terrified after years of bombing also had a natural instinct to flee the danger zone.

The U.S. government made hasty plans to evacuate Americans plus current and former Vietnamese employees, their families, and other South Vietnamese whose lives were clearly in danger. In the frantic atmosphere of April 29-30, desperate Vietnamese stormed the gates of the U.S. Embassy and clung to helicopter doors. Tens of thousands of "high risk" South Vietnamese were left behind, while others who were not on the lists (such as soldiers) managed to get American transportation or escape on their own.

April 30, 1975, would later become known as the "Day of Anguish" among first wave Vietnamese Americans. Typically, they had less than twenty-four hours to prepare to leave. Some did not even know where they were going. Most thought that they were only leaving temporarily and would be able to return to Vietnam as soon as the Communist government fell.

The "pull factors" that brought 125,000 Vietnamese to the United States in 1975 are more complicated. There was much debate in the U.S. government about what America's obligations were to the South Vietnamese people. President Gerald Ford believed that the United States was morally responsible for them because of America's role in the war and because they were "voting with their feet" against Communism. The 1965 Immigration and Nationality Act had done away with favoritism to immigrants from Europe, making it easier for Asians and Latin Americans to come to America. Congress passed the 1975 Indochinese Refugee Act, which allowed up to 200,000 Vietnamese and other Indochinese to enter the United States quickly under special parole status (that is, without having to go through the normal immigration process). Under pressure from the President and the press, Congress also approved $405 million in resettlement aid for the refugees.

RELUCTANCE TO HELP

Congress had been reluctant to take these moves due to negative public opinion. A Gallup opinion poll showed 54 percent of Americans against this action and only 36 percent in favor of admitting large numbers of Vietnamese refugees. What prompted this reluctance? First of all, 1975 was a bad year for the economy with almost one in every ten Americans out of work. Many Americans feared that refugees would take away their jobs, or that government aid to the refugees would mean less help for American veterans and the unemployed. In addition, some Americans were tired of hearing about an unpopular war and did not want the United States to have any more responsibility for it. Finally, prejudice against Asians in general or Vietnamese in particular may have played a role.

This climate of public opinion continued to influence U.S. government policy once the refugees reached American soil. They were strongly urged to resettle in other, third countries or consider returning to Vietnam. About 1,500 chose to return. Only about 6,500 were able to find third countries that would take them, mainly Canada, France, and Australia. The world considered the refugees America's problem. And the American government was determined to resettle them as quickly as possible with the least possible economic impact on American communities.

RESETTLEMENT EFFORTS

The refugees were moved from the island of Guam to four resettlement camps in California (Camp Pendleton), Arkansas (Fort Chaffee), Florida (Eglin Air Force Base), and Pennsylvania (Fort Indiantown Gap). They lived 25 to a tent or 100 to a barracks in these instant cities of 25,000 people. The American-run camps were complete with large mess halls, recreation activities, religious services, and their own newspapers. They also offered schools for the children and English or practical orientation classes for the adults. Classes were well attended but reportedly left the Vietnamese confused since they tried to impose American ways without much understanding of or tolerance for Vietnamese culture. In any case, the main business for the refugees in the camps was waiting in lines. They had to be given security checks, identification numbers, medical exams, and interviews. They also had to be assigned to one of nine private voluntary agencies (called VOLAGs) which would help them find a sponsor within forty-five days.

The VOLAGs were organizations with years of experience helping immigrants and refugees from other countries. Most were religious, such as the U.S. Catholic Conference, Lutheran Immigration and Refugee Service, and Hebrew Immigrant Aid Society. They were supposed to match up each Vietnamese with an American church, family, or company sponsor that would agree to take financial and moral responsibility for them until the refugees could support themselves. This meant giving them food, clothing, and housing, and helping them find jobs and schooling (nearly half the first-wave refugees were under the age of eighteen). The government gave a resettlement grant of $500 per refugee, but this covered only a fraction of the costs.

The American sponsorship program had mixed results. Since it was all arranged on short notice before sponsors and

Catholic parishes across the country opened their hearts and arms to welcome the refugees. Sponsored by the U.S. Catholic Conference, this church represents the many VOLAGs that reached out to help the new arrivals.

refugees could meet personally, neither the Americans nor the Vietnamese knew what to expect. While still in the camps, many refugees rejected sponsorship situations that would require them to split up the family or go to a cold climate. Cultural differences often caused friction once they were matched up. Some sponsors felt that the refugees were ungrateful for all the sacrifices that were being made for them, or were too dependent on charity. Some refugees felt insulted that everything was managed for them by others and that they were pushed into low-status jobs. Company sponsors, such as candy factories or fish processing plants, frequently used the refugees as cheap labor in violation of American labor laws. For example, they paid the refugees the minimum wage of $2.10 per hour or less, but then deducted the cost of their room and board.

By the end of 1975, the first-wave refugees were all resettled with American sponsors. The government had succeeded in its goal of making sure they were spread out, rather than concentrated in certain parts of the country, so as not to be an economic threat to any one American community. About two thirds of Vietnamese men and one quarter of the women above the age of sixteen were working. Most were in very low-paying jobs with no possibility of advancement (see "What They Do"). Households were large (averaging five or more people) and increasingly, family members had to go on welfare to make ends meet. Still, the government planned to phase out its aid program to the refugees by 1977, when it was assumed they would be self-supporting.

NEW PROBLEMS IN VIETNAM: THE SECOND-WAVE

The second wave of Vietnamese refugees beginning in late 1978 once again took America by surprise. Many Vietnamese had stayed in their country after 1975, hoping to resume their lives in peace. Large numbers of them—even some with no

Patterns of East Asian Refugee Flight

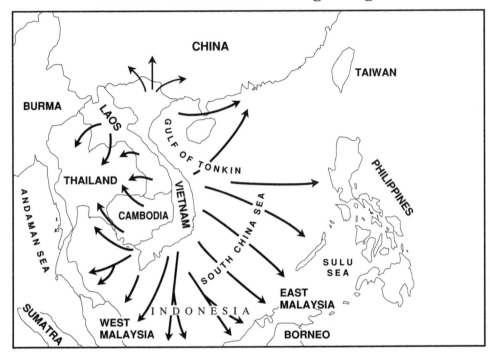

obvious ties to the Americans or the former South Vietnamese government—were sent by the Communists to reeducation camps. Here they were forced to do hard labor and taught to think according to Communist beliefs. Four million city dwellers were moved to isolated "new economic zones" to work as farmers to help ease the country's food shortages. The middle and upper classes were also hurt by the government's seizure of 30,000 private businesses and by the change in currency that made many people's savings suddenly worthless. As if all this was not hard enough, in 1978 and 1979 there were devastating floods in many Vietnamese agricultural areas and the government called a new draft to recruit soldiers for its war in Cambodia.

Conditions became especially intolerable for the two million ethnic Chinese in Vietnam. They had long been resented for dominating trade and for living with their own ways in tight-knit communities such as Cholon outside Saigon. After Vietnam invaded Cambodia in December, 1978, China (an ally of Cambodia) invaded Vietnam's northern border in early 1979. The Vietnamese government made it clear that ethnic Chinese were under suspicion and no longer welcome in the country. Their businesses were seized, their schools closed, and curfews were imposed to restrict their activities. From 1978 to 1979, about 250,000 Chinese Vietnamese fled overland to China, where many still live on resettlement farms.

Others paid up to $2,000 each in gold to leave the country by boat. The Vietnamese government apparently encouraged and profited from this practice. It is thought that two thirds of the 85,000 boat people who left Vietnam in late 1978 were Chinese. Some Vietnamese faked their papers to appear Chinese in order to leave on the same boats. Others escaped illegally by night in small fishing boats, fearing arrest.

THE BOAT PEOPLE

Whether ethnic Chinese or Vietnamese, legal or illegal, once at sea these refugees were boat people exposed to the same horrors. Their rickety and overcrowded ships became known as "floating coffins." They ran out of fuel, food, and water, and were forced to eat seagulls to survive. About half of the boat people were children or teenagers, who suffered greatly from what they witnessed. One fourteen-year-old boy named Hieu told of seeing several of his boat mates shot by Communists on an island, with survivors drifting for ten days without fuel or water, eating only a spoonful of rice per day, until they were finally rescued by a Japanese ship. Worse stories of rape, murder, and ruthless theft are told by boat people who were repeatedly attacked by pirates.

The boat people hoped to find safe refuge in Hong Kong,

P. Deloche, courtesy of United Nations High Commission for Refugees

Adrift in the South China Sea, these Vietnamese boat people were saved in time.

Indonesia, Malaysia, the Philippines, or Thailand. But as more and more of them arrived, these countries of first asylum were unwilling or unable to take on the burden of the refugees. Their boats were left in limbo in the ports or turned back to sea, with local ships refusing to rescue them. Sometimes the refugees were crowded into makeshift camps such as Pilau Bidong in Malaysia, a quarter mile of rock island where some 42,000 people lived without any sanitary facilities.

The plight of the boat people captured world attention and sympathy. But individual countries and the United Nations were slow to take action. The U.S. government had assumed that by admitting small numbers of Vietnamese refugees in 1976 and 1977, it would be "mopping up" the refugee problem. Faced with the boat people crisis in 1978-1979, the U.S. Navy and private charitable organizations eventually sent rescue ships to the area. President Jimmy Carter increased the numbers of Vietnamese that could come to America under special parole, citing humanitarian reasons.

The Refugee Act of 1980 changed American law to define refugees for the first time according to United Nations standards as people leaving their countries because of persecution, or reason to fear persecution because of their race, religion, nationality, political beliefs, or social class. Now, instead of having to issue special paroles, the United States could admit refugees automatically and quickly. Accordingly, 1980 and 1981 were peak years of arrival for second wave Vietnamese in the United States (95,000 and 86,000 respectively). The new law also helped 105,000 Cambodians escaping from mass killings to come to the United States between 1979 and 1981.

IMMIGRATION TO CANADA

There were new pull factors in Canada as well. Only 8,000 Vietnamese lived there in 1978. The Canadian Immigration Act of 1976 (put into effect in 1978) set new definitions for refugees, treating the Indochinese as a special class who did not have to prove that they had been persecuted. When the boat *Hai Hong* was turned away from Malaysia in 1978, Canada offered to take 600 of the 2,500 refugees on board. Eventually, the Canadian government took in 45,000 more Vietnamese boat people from 1979 to 1980—the largest intake for any country of comparable population size.

As in the United States with the first wave, there was strong public sentiment in Canada against receiving this large wave of refugees (51 percent opposed, 36 percent in favor in a 1979 opinion poll). However, Canada's unique formula for admitting and sponsoring the refugees also rallied immense popular

support. Each refugee sponsored directly by the government
was supposed to be matched by private sponsorships by a
church, organization, work place, or group of at least five
neighbors. The more private sponsors there were, the more
refugees the government could theoretically sponsor.
Grassroots groups such as Project 4000 and Operation Lifeline
sprang up and helped organize nearly 5,500 sponsorship
groups within six months. Government-sponsored refugees
were supported for six months while learning English and
being placed in jobs. Private sponsor groups set up various
committees to deal with refugee needs and are generally
thought to have given the refugees a more generous and
helpful start in their adjustment to Canadian life. Like the
United States in 1975, the Canadian government in 1980
expected to quickly wind up its obligations to Indochinese
refugees.

THE CONTINUING EXODUS

Both the United States and Canada accepted far fewer
Vietnamese refugees after 1981-1982 (see pages 51 and 52).
But people continued to escape Vietnam and to crowd
inadequate refugee camps in Asia throughout the 1980's. In
order to block the tide of boat people at its source, the U.S.
government pressured the Vietnamese government to allow
more legal emigration. The Orderly Departure Program was
set up to bring Vietnamese directly from Vietnam to America
as immigrants, rather than refugees, in order to reunite them
with their families. This program has usually required long
waits for the Vietnamese—of the 500,000 applications on file
in 1985, only 300 were processed per week—but has managed
to bring 66,000 immigrants to America since 1983. The
Amerasian Homecoming Act of 1987 made it possible to bring
over 46,000 Amerasian teenagers and their families under a
special arrangement: They were processed as immigrants but

were also eligible for government refugee benefits. Another new program provides for the legal immigration of former South Vietnamese political prisoners, with 7,000 expected in the United States in 1990.

World opinion has become less and less sympathetic to the boat people as their crisis continues. In the late 1980's, Hong Kong, Malaysia, and Thailand closed their doors to the Vietnamese. They considered the new boat people not refugees but "economic migrants" (people who move in search of better economic opportunities). However, a United Nations survey in 1987 found that more than two-thirds of the recent escapees were either ethnic Chinese or had been through reeducation camps. More than 100,000 Vietnamese remained in Southeast Asian refugee camps in 1990—the highest total since the height of the boat people crisis in 1979.

IMMIGRANTS HELP THEIR COUNTRYMEN

If governments seem to have forgotten those who still want to leave Vietnam, Vietnamese Americans have not. They started organizations to promote their cause in the 1980's such as Coalition for the Protection of Vietnamese Boat Refugees and Families of Political Prisoners Association. The Indochina Resource Action Center in Washington, D.C., continues to lobby Congress on behalf of the thousands of people who have been displaced by changes in Southeast Asia. Vietnamese families are among the main sponsors of new refugees and immigrants to the United States, while a network of private Canadian sponsorship committees is steadily bringing over more people from the camps.

The United States continued to admit Southeast Asians as its largest category of refugees from 1980 to 1990, but in numbers well below the maximums set by law for each year. Government funding of the Office of Refugee Resettlement has been cut over the years from a high of $902 million in

1981 to a low of $340 million in 1987. Whereas a Vietnamese boat person who arrived in 1979 could receive government financial help for up to three years, a refugee arriving in 1989 was only eligible for one year of aid. Current government programs do not meet the needs of the continuing stream of newcomers, according to Vietnamese-American leaders. But the community fears that if it asks for more government services, the government will cut the numbers of Vietnamese allowed to enter the United States. Bringing over those they left behind remains the highest priority.

WHEN THEY CAME

The vast majority of Vietnamese came to the United States and Canada since 1975. However, about 20,000 immigrated to the United States as wives and children of American servicemen during the Vietnam War from 1965 to 1975. Canada had a population of about 1,000 Vietnamese before 1975, mostly students and professionals.

Vietnamese immigration can be understood in terms of three waves of settlement, as described in earlier chapters. The first wave came in 1975 immediately after the fall of Saigon to the Communists. This was the largest single year's admission of Vietnamese refugees into the United States (125,000), but was much less significant for Canada (2,281). The second wave began after the boat people crisis of late 1978. It brought large numbers of Vietnamese to Canada for the first time in 1979 and 1980 (45,000), and even larger numbers to the United States from 1978 to 1982 (280,500). Since that time, arrivals of Vietnamese refugees in both the United States and Canada have declined considerably. The third wave (1982 to the present) has been more tightly restricted by government policy.

The figures given below for the United States and Canada represent only those Vietnamese admitted as refugees rather than as regular immigrants (see table on page 52). More than 78,000 Vietnamese came to the United States as official immigrants from 1971 to 1989, according to the Immigration and Naturalization Service. These figures include people being reunited with their families as well as the recent influx of young Amerasians. Year by year figures that clearly separate

51

immigrants from refugee admissions, however, are not available for either the United States or Canada. It should also be remembered that not all Vietnamese Americans came to America as refugees or immigrants from Vietnam. An estimated 200,000 to 250,000 Vietnamese children have been born in the United States since 1975.

ADMISSIONS OF VIETNAMESE REFUGEES TO THE UNITED STATES AND CANADA: 1975-1990

Year	Refugees Admitted	
	United States	*Canada*
1975	125,000	2,281
1976	3,200	2,291
1977	1,900	459
1978	11,100	659
1979	44,500	19,710
1980	95,200	25,337
1981	86,100	7,455
1982	43,656	3,831
1983	23,459	3,056
1984	24,818	3,466
1985	25,457	4,281
1986	22,796	3,880
1987	23,012	3,966
1988	17,654	4,653
1989	22,664	5,423
1990	27,714	5,166
Total:	595,300	95,914

Sources: United States figures are from Office of Refugee Resettlement, U.S. Department of Health and Human Services, and Bureau for Refugee Programs, Department of State. Canadian figures are from Immigration Canada.

Note: United States figures correspond to numbers for each federal fiscal year (July through June).

WHERE THEY LIVE

When the first wave of Vietnamese came to America in 1975, where they lived depended on where they found a sponsor. This was partly affected by the location of the resettlement camps in Arkansas, California, Florida, and Pennsylvania, since Americans from these regions who worked at the camps often became sponsors. Five state governments (Iowa, Maine, New Mexico, Oklahoma, and Washington) also sponsored limited numbers of the first-wave refugees.

The largest groups of first-wave Vietnamese were resettled in the big states of California (27,199) and Texas (9,130), with 3,500 to 7,000 each resettled in Pennsylvania, Florida, Washington, Illinois, New York, and Louisiana. It was government policy to resettle no more than 3,000 Vietnamese in any one area so as to minimize economic and social problems for Americans already living there. This, however, created hardship for the Vietnamese: They had to adjust to their new lives without the benefit of a supportive community around them.

As soon as they could, many Vietnamese in small towns and isolated areas moved to larger cities. This movement after their initial immigration is called secondary migration. It was prompted by the refugees' needs for better jobs, homes close to relatives, warmer climate, more generous welfare benefits, and the services of Vietnamese communities. By 1979, 43 percent of the Southeast Asian refugee population was concentrated in two states: California and Texas. This pattern has held true through the arrival of many thousands more Vietnamese in the second and third waves.

VIETNAMESE IN CALIFORNIA AND TEXAS

Nearly half of all Vietnamese Americans today live in California and Texas (see table below). They were attracted to key cities such as Los Angeles and Dallas by family ties and the presence of strong Vietnamese communities where they could feel at home. California, with its mild climate, plentiful jobs, and good social services, has been the most popular American destination of immigrants of all nationalities since 1971. It is home to one-third of all Asian Americans, with one out of every ten Californians being of Asian descent.

The three biggest Vietnamese-American communities are

STATES WITH A SOUTHEAST ASIAN REFUGEE POPULATION OF 20,000 OR MORE: 1990

California	376,500
Texas	71,400
Washington	44,700
Minnesota	34,800*
New York	34,100
Pennsylvania	30,200
Illinois	30,000
Massachusetts	29,900*
Virginia	24,100
Oregon	21,100

Source: Office of Refugee Resettlement
Note: Vietnamese refugees make up about two-thirds of the total Southeast Asian refugee population in the United States (No separate figures are available for Vietnamese populations by state.) Figures marked with an asterisk (*) indicate totals for which the Vietnamese population is likely to be less than two-thirds, since there are large numbers of Cambodian and Laotian refugees in these states.

California's Orange County (140,000), Los Angeles County (100,000), and Santa Clara County (75,000). The San Jose area in Santa Clara County, south of San Francisco, offered cheap housing, plentiful and well-paying jobs in the electronics industry, and affordable education at good community colleges. Today many Vietnamese there own their own homes, run businesses downtown, and enjoy ten local Vietnamese newspapers. In Los Angeles, the Vietnamese are one among many new immigrant groups who are changing the face of the city; for example, ethnic Chinese have bought up many of the old Cantonese Chinese businesses in Chinatown. Orange County's Little Saigon, located in the communities of Garden Grove and Westminster, south of Los Angeles, is pointed to proudly as the "refugees' capital" with its thousands of Vietnamese businesses, services, and organizations. But like the Vietnamese population in the United States as a whole, Orange County Vietnamese are a diverse group, ranging from the wealthy few to many poor families.

The Vietnamese in Texas are perhaps best known for their communities along the Gulf of Mexico. Both experienced fishermen and unskilled factory workers went there to work in the fishing industry. They often worked long hours and pooled their earnings in order to buy their own boats. In some areas, the enterprising Vietnamese with their different fishing and cultural practices were resented as competition by local fishermen (see page 67). In 1979 in Seadrift, Texas, a fight broke out and an American fisherman was killed by two Vietnamese brothers; three Vietnamese boats and one house were set on fire by angry locals, and 150 Vietnamese left the town in fear. Despite this and other hostile incidents, Vietnamese continue to work and live in small Gulf Coast towns in Texas, Louisiana, Mississippi, Alabama, and Florida.

VIETNAMESE IN OTHER STATES

Other Vietnamese communities in the United States have their special character and "pull factors" which brought Vietnamese there. For example, Washington, D.C., and the surrounding suburbs in Maryland and Virginia have always attracted well-educated Vietnamese because of the prospect of international or U.S. government jobs. Vietnamese Catholic priests such as Father Manger at the Fort Chaffee, Arkansas, refugee camp gathered their followers and transplanted entire villages to places such as Beaufort-Port Arthur, Texas, and the community of Versailles outside New Orleans, Louisiana. Hundreds of Montagnards (a hill tribe from Vietnam known for their loyal anti-Communist fighters) were brought to Greensboro, North Carolina, in 1986 through their connections with U.S. military sponsors there. More than 1,200 people of the Tai Dam hill tribe sponsored by the state of Iowa are still living there.

It is common for Vietnamese, especially new arrivals and those with low-paying jobs, to live in inner-city areas such as the Uptown neighborhood of Chicago or East Dallas' Little Asia. The elderly are often afraid to walk the streets of these neighborhoods, where they fear being robbed and harassed. The East Dallas Police Storefront was set up to offer Vietnamese a crime hot line, as well as a food bank and youth recreation activities. The Vietnamese must compete with other minorities for scarce resources in poor urban areas, sometimes leading to tensions. In 1979, a riot broke out at a Denver, Colorado, housing project when Mexican Americans who had been on a waiting list for apartments learned that Vietnamese refugees would be given apartments ahead of them.

IN THE HEARTLAND: OKLAHOMA CITY

While no single Vietnamese-American community is typical, the case of Oklahoma City in the American heartland is

SOUTHEAST ASIAN REFUGEE POPULATION BY STATE AND REGION, 1989

West		Southeast	
Alaska	200	Alabama	3,400
California	363,800	Arkansas	3,200
Hawaii	7,900	Florida	15,700
Idaho	1,900	Georgia	12,000
Montana	1,000	Kentucky	3,100
Oregon	20,500	Louisiana	15,300
Washington	43,000	Mississippi	1,900
Wyoming	200	North Carolina	6,900
		South Carolina	2,500
		Tennessee	6,300
		Virginia	23,100
		West Virginia	400

Southwest		Middle Atlantic	
Arizona	7,600	Delaware	300
Colorado	12,400	District of Columbia	1,800
Nevada	2,500	Maryland	10,800
New Mexico	2,300	New Jersey	8,400
Oklahoma	9,200	New York	33,100
Texas	68,400	Pennsylvania	29,200
Utah	9,200		

Midwest		New England	
Illinois	29,300	Connecticut	8,200
Indiana	4,400	Maine	1,700
Iowa	10,200	Massachusetts	29,500
Kansas	10,800	New Hampshire	900
Michigan	12,500	Rhode Island	7,600
Minnesota	33,800	Vermont	700
Missouri	8,400		
Nebraska	2,700		
North Dakota	1,000		
Ohio	12,600		
South Dakota	1,100		
Wisconsin	15,300		

Source: Office of Refugee Resettlement, U.S. Department of Health and Human Services

Note: Separate figures for Vietnamese population are unavailable.

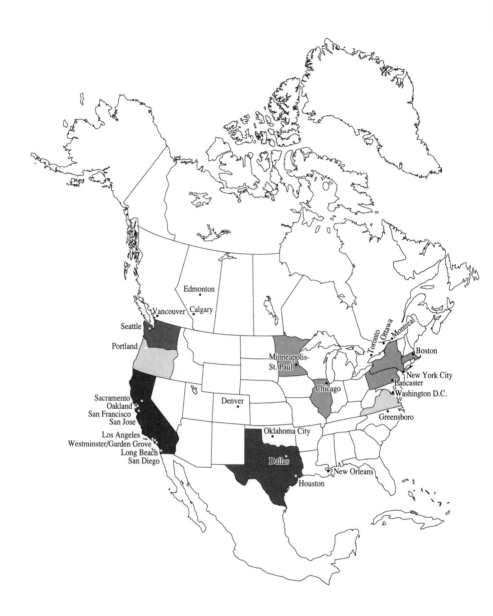

Edmonton

Vancouver Calgary

Seattle

Portland

Minneapolis-
St. Paul

Toronto
Ottawa
Montreal

Boston

New York City

Lancaster

Washington D.C.

Chicago

Sacramento
Oakland
San Francisco
San Jose

Denver

Greensboro

Los Angeles
Westminster/Garden Grove
Long Beach
San Diego

Oklahoma City

Dallas

New Orleans

Houston

revealing. In 1984, it had about 7,500 Vietnamese: Half of these residents were first-wave refugees, 40 percent were boat people, and 10 percent were official immigrants. Most of the Vietnamese there worked in factories and wanted their children to go to college. They tended to live first in the Northwest part of the inner city, and then bought houses in the suburbs after several years. The local Vietnamese American Association, which discouraged welfare and offered social services to help the Vietnamese become self-sufficient as soon as possible, became a model for federally funded programs.

About half of this Vietnamese community was Buddhist, with the other half split between Catholics (28 percent) and Protestants. While the vast majority of Vietnamese had lived in extended family households in Vietnam, only 8 percent did so in Oklahoma City. Many described themselves as having a "half and half" way of life: American-style at work or school, but more traditionally Vietnamese at home. For example, most spoke English and ate sandwiches and sodas with their coworkers or classmates, but spoke Vietnamese and ate Vietnamese meals at home. Parents were strict about children studying and expected to be consulted about who they would marry. Some traditional Vietnamese *le hoi* engagement ceremonies were still conducted in the home; wedding customs varied widely, but usually included restaurant receptions.

Rather than having home altars, the Oklahoma City Vietnamese tended to pray to their ancestors at community altars at the Buddhist temple. The only large community events were Tet and Mid-Autumn festival celebrations. While Vietnamese in bigger communities have a more varied and bustling community life, they share the sense of being "half and half"—one foot still in Vietnam, one in America—with their Oklahoma City compatriots.

COMMUNITIES IN CANADA

Less information is available on Vietnamese living patterns in Canada, where strong communities only formed after the 1979-1980 second wave. By the 1986 census, the largest concentrations of Vietnamese were found in Montreal and Toronto, followed by Calgary, Vancouver, and Edmonton (see table below). The province of Quebec, which has its own immigration policy and a natural interest in the French-influenced culture of Vietnam, took a leading role in sponsoring refugees. Canadian Vietnamese, even more so than those in the United States, are predominantly ethnic Chinese. Although older Chinese-Canadian organizations were active in helping the Chinese Vietnamese get settled, the two communities have remained separate.

VIETNAMESE POPULATION OF SELECTED CANADIAN CITIES AND PROVINCES: 1986

Ontario	17,155
Toronto	10,275
Ottawa	2,085
Quebec	15,865
Montreal	14,035
Alberta	9,625
Calgary	4,595
Edmonton	4,115
British Columbia	5,740
Vancouver	4,307

Source: Statistics Canada (1986 census)

Note: Compared with the total number of refugees admitted through 1986, these census figures appear to have greatly undercounted Vietnamese Canadians.

WHAT THEY DO

Liem Huu Nguyen never dreamed he would be a lawyer in the United States. He grew up in a poor peasant family in central Vietnam and arrived in America in 1975 at the age of eighteen. He studied law at Oklahoma State University, and now counts many young Vietnamese among his clients in San Jose.

My Hanh Do always wanted to be a lawyer but gave up on the idea after coming to the United States because of her trouble with English. Instead, she got a scholarship in electrical engineering and now designs software for the well-known Bell Laboratories.

Thanh Ngoc Nguyen, who came to Houston as a boat person, has three jobs. He is a draftsman by day, a video rental store owner by night, and an installer of security alarms on the weekends. He works eighteen-hour days, seven days a week.

After working for various refugee agencies, Han Tho and Mary Touch started their own chain of French croissant bakeries in Sacramento, California. They, too, work long hours and have helped other refugees start bakeries.

These are just some of the Vietnamese success stories in America. The Vietnamese are best known for their small businesses and for their role in the electronics, engineering, and health fields. But like other immigrants, they actually work at a variety of jobs and professions. Because of their refugee experience, short time in America, and cultural background, their work situation is also uniquely Vietnamese.

A hard-working Vietnamese-American seamstress, in Virginia, contributes to her family's finances.

FINDING A JOB, MAKING A LIVING

The work history of the first-wave Vietnamese is one of dramatic contrasts. Most were working within a year of being resettled in the United States in 1975. But one-third of these people earned less than the minimum wage (then $2.10 per hour) and the average family income was still below the poverty level in 1977. More than 60 percent of Vietnamese who had been white-collar (office or sales) workers in Vietnam were doing blue-collar (manual) work in the United States. It was not uncommon for a former South Vietnamese army general to be a waiter or a former bank manager a janitor. Adjusting to a lower social status was very difficult for those first-wave refugees who had been part of their country's upper classes; some refused to take jobs they felt were below their dignity.

With hard work, most of the early refugees eventually established themselves in better jobs (see table on page 64). Doctors and lawyers passed the exams for American certification; others sought new lines of work. For example, a former South Vietnamese Navy officer became a math teacher and eventually an assistant high school principal in Virginia, while his wife worked as a medical technician. By 1985, the first-wave Vietnamese had incomes equal to or better than the American average.

The longer Vietnamese have been in the United States and the better their English, the higher their income. As noted in the chapters "The Vietnamese in North America" and "Why America?" the second- and third-wave Vietnamese came to America with less education, poorer knowledge of English, and fewer job skills than the early refugees. In a 1984 study of Chinese Vietnamese in five American cities, half were found to be working low status jobs that left their families below the poverty level. In 1987, Vietnamese immigrants who had arrived between 1976 and 1979 were earning an average of

63

OCCUPATIONAL STATUS OF VIETNAMESE REFUGEES WHO ARRIVED IN THE UNITED STATES BETWEEN 1985 AND 1989

Type of occupation	Percentage	
	Vietnam, pre-1985	*United States, 1989*
White Collar	28.2	13.4
Professional/managerial	6.7	1.7
Sales/clerical	21.5	11.7
Blue Collar	18.4	64.8
Skilled	12.6	23.2
Semiskilled	5.2	34.4
Unskilled	0.6	7.2
Other	53.4	21.6
Service workers	6.1	20.3
Farming/fishing	47.3	1.3

Source: Refugee Resettlement Program 1990 Report to Congress, U.S. Department of Health and Human Services Office of Refugee Resettlement

$14,000, $3,000 less than the American median income. In 1989, 55 percent of Vietnamese in the United States above the age of sixteen were working as compared to 66 percent of Americans. Not surprisingly, the figure was lower (37 percent) for those refugees who had been in America four years or less.

THE STRUGGLE FOR SELF-SUFFICIENCY

From 1975 to the present, refugee agencies and sponsors in both the United States and Canada have urged the Vietnamese to take any available job as quickly as possible. Resettlement programs have stressed job placement rather than retraining for new jobs in the hope that this would allow Vietnamese to become self-sufficient faster. As a result, many Vietnamese have became stuck in low-paying, dead-end jobs with no time to improve their English or skills so as to find better positions. This situation, plus the large size of their households, has driven about one-third of Vietnamese Americans to take cash assistance (welfare) from the government.

Successful Vietnamese professionals from the first wave or those who have gone from "rags to riches" get the publicity. But what kinds of work do most Vietnamese Americans do today? The majority hold blue-collar jobs, for example, assembling televisions in Lancaster, Pennsylvania, or electronic parts in California's Silicon Valley. Others are in service jobs in restaurants, hotels, hospitals, and transportation. Newcomers rely on sponsors or relatives to help them find these jobs, which still tend to be very different from the types of jobs they held in Vietnam (see table on page 64).

VIETNAMESE ENTREPRENEURS

A Vietnamese shop in Arlington, Virginia, has the name Dat Hung (Attaining Prosperity). More and more Vietnamese seek this goal by starting their own businesses. These tend to be small, family-run, and geared to Vietnamese customers. Typical examples are restaurants, Oriental grocery stores, tailor shops, laundries, and beauty salons. In the 1986 Vietnamese Business Directory for Los Angeles and Orange Counties, more than 1,000 businesses are listed. Besides restaurants and markets, the directory listings include numerous jewelry stores, auto repair shops, and insurance offices, plus a handful of computer stores, dancing schools, and photographers. Some traditional businesses transfer well from Vietnam to large Vietnamese-American communities, such as Chinese medicinal herb shops, cultural stores with Vietnamese books and tapes, or the daily home delivery of hot Vietnamese meals.

Chinese Vietnamese are prominent among these new entrepreneurs in America. It was they who owned small shops in Vietnam, particularly in the food business; their contacts

65

This Chinese-Vietnamese grocery in New York City is a thriving business.

with food exporters in Asia continue to serve them well. In California, American-born Chinese often sell their mom-and-pop corner groceries to ethnic Chinese from Vietnam.

In Southern California's Little Saigon, Vietnamese businesses made more than $300 million in sales in 1985. The Vietnamese Chamber of Commerce has branches around the United States to promote more Vietnamese entrepreneurs. They offer training workshops and publications in Vietnamese on various aspects of starting and managing a business. Other groups such as the Vietnamese American Association in Oklahoma City hope to decrease competition between Vietnamese restaurants and markets by encouraging a greater variety of businesses such as convenience stores, liquor stores, and video arcades that also attract non-Vietnamese customers.

WEALTH FROM THE SEA

Another line of work in which Vietnamese Americans have enjoyed a sense of independence and being their own boss is fishing. The fishermen's experience shows how cultural differences can greatly affect the workplace. For example, Vietnamese fishermen tended to use family members to work around the clock, saving their pay quickly to buy up secondhand boats; they also fished areas intensively with oversize nets or traps set close together. These practices, which would have been normal for the fishing fleet in Vietnam, were resented by Americans in the more tightly regulated American shrimp and crab fishing business. Vietnamese fishermen were also criticized for eating the undersize shrimp they caught and even catching pelicans (protected under U.S. law)—customs foreign to the Americans. Misunderstandings and violence resulted in some towns on the Gulf Coast (see page 55). In Florida, two counties passed laws forbidding the use of oversize gillnets in an attempt to restrain Vietnamese fishing. In the San Francisco Bay area, Vietnamese fishermen recently

won a battle to make an exception in a law which banned
noncitizens from owning commercial fishing boats.

WORK AND VIETNAMESE VALUES

The Vietnamese fishermen are motivated by a strong work
ethic which has long been a part of their culture. Vietnamese
factory workers have likewise been resented by their American
coworkers because of their short lunch breaks and long
overtime. As newcomers struggling to rise their standard of
living, "we have to work hard, harder than the others,"
according to a refugee agency director in Long Beach,
California. Many Vietnamese work double shifts or two jobs
because they must make dollars stretch to support larger
families, sponsor elderly relatives, or send money back to
Vietnam.

"One house, one cooking pot," says an old Vietnamese
proverb. All who work generally put their wages into a
common household fund and ask permission from the others
when they want to make a major purchase, change jobs, or go
to college. Rather than living beyond their means on credit as
Americans tend to do, the Vietnamese save carefully and
willingly make sacrifices for their long-term goals. Already by
the 1980 U.S. census, more than one-quarter of them owned
their homes—historically a sign of having "made it" in
America.

CONTRIBUTIONS

TO SOCIETY

With their dedication to hard work and the high value they place on education, the Vietnamese have been giving their talents to American society for more than fifteen years. Their achievements in schools and universities, as well as in science, technology, and business are held up as an inspiration to other newcomers. These accomplishments are a tribute to the strong family values and adaptability of Vietnamese culture. They are also a sign of the unique characteristics of the first wave of refugees, many of whom were already skilled, well-educated, urban, and Westernized when they arrived.

Some Vietnamese have made their mark on American life as famous individuals (see "Famous Vietnamese Americans"). The Vietnamese as a people have had a broader impact on their adopted country. Like immigrants before them, they have found ways to help themselves while benefiting the society in general. They have brought their industriousness and determination to sectors of the economy that other Americans abandoned. For example, they revived declining city neighborhoods such as downtown San Jose by opening businesses and community institutions. On the Gulf Coast, they are credited with saving the ailing crab and shrimp industries and repopulating small towns such as Bayou La Batre, Alabama (now one-third Vietnamese after the departure of American fishermen).

Stanford University's student/athlete Tuan Van Le reflects the Vietnamese-American commitment to education and to excellence in all areas of endeavor.

NEW CULTURAL HORIZONS

Culturally, the Vietnamese have added yet another dimension to the American melting pot and the Canadian multicultural mosaic. They brought with them a whole new set of foods, customs, and art forms. These contributions are slowly becoming more familiar to non-Vietnamese at restaurants, festivals, school assemblies, and elsewhere. But the cultural impact of the Vietnamese in America has meant much more than just another kind of egg roll to sample.

The influx of large numbers of Vietnamese Buddhists and the establishment of new temples have had a tremendous effect on the Buddhist movement in America. Vietnamese monks and nuns brought leadership and scholarship to Buddhist communities where membership (especially among Japanese Americans) had been steadily decreasing. Temples such as Chua Viet Nam in Los Angeles now offer most services and activities in English so as to reach out to Buddhists of all nationalities and to ensure the continued vitality of their religion in America.

Some Vietnamese have devoted themselves to teaching Americans about their culture and way of life, most often through books, essays, and intercultural workshops. One unusual example is the Trung Van Vo family, which came to Los Angeles in 1986 with thirty-five traditional Vietnamese musical instruments and hundreds of cassettes and books in their luggage. The seven Vo children, ages 7 to 23, had spent the years since 1975 in secret study with the masters of Vietnamese music and dance. They learned to perform a vast repertoire from funeral ritual music to comic opera scenes, while their parents wrote and recited poetry. The family's self-proclaimed mission in America is to preserve this heritage which they fear is being lost in their native Vietnam. Their California audiences are enthusiastic not only about the impressive variety of music the Vos perform from all regions

71

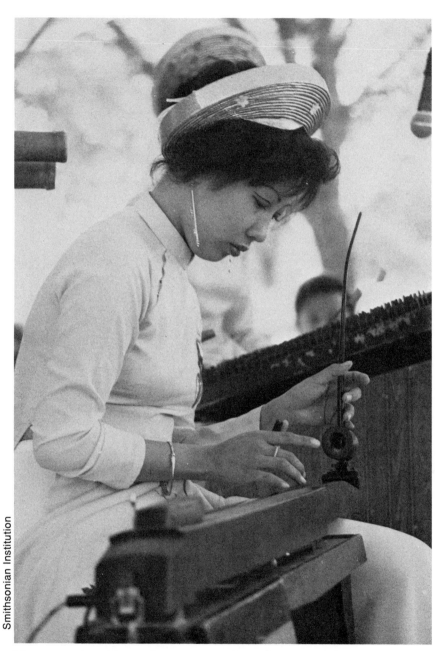

Vietnamese American performs on a traditional instrument from her home country during the Festival of American Folklife, in Washington, D.C.

of Vietnam, but about the solo by the youngest boy Viet on the eerie, one-stringed monochord of the theme from the American movie, *The Godfather*. This kind of cross-cultural contact suggests how Vietnamese and American culture can influence and enrich each other.

A DIFFERENT PERSPECTIVE ON THE WAR

The Vietnamese presence in the United States also challenges Americans to see beyond their own view of the divisive Vietnam War. Many Vietnamese Americans suffer from a "Vietnam Syndrome" quite different from that of American veterans. They feel betrayed by both the South Vietnamese and American governments for failing to stop the Communist takeover of their country, and they are angry with recent books and movies in the United States which portray the Vietnamese in minor roles as victims of the war. More Vietnamese are telling their own stories now, as in the memoir *When Heaven and Earth Changed Places* by Le Ly Hayslip. "We obeyed both sides and wound up pleasing neither," she writes of the war years. "We were people in the middle. . . . We knew little of democracy and even less about communism. For most of us it was a fight for independence." Likewise, American students who have never lived through a war have learned about its horrors firsthand from the essays and art work of their Vietnamese classmates.

In 1985, ten years after the fall of Saigon and the arrival of the first-wave refugees, *Newsweek* magazine issued a thirty-five-page special edition on the legacy of the war. Only one page covered Vietnamese Americans, painting a rosy picture of "rags to riches" success and gratitude for freedom in the United States. Gradually, Americans may come to see that the real Vietnamese-American experience is a lot more complicated. As Dung Nguyen, a twenty-three-year-old engineer, comments in a recent book on new Americans,

"Physically, life in the United States is very comfortable. But I can't help feeling sad thinking of people in Vietnam who work ten to twelve hours a day and still don't have enough to eat. How do I deserve being so well-off? I have a brother and sister in Vietnam. Sometimes I feel very guilty." The most in-depth study of Vietnamese Americans to date is called, significantly, *Hearts of Sorrow*.

LESSONS IN TOLERANCE

All this is part of an eye-opening education for North Americans about the wider world, especially the problems and culture of a poor, faraway country such as Vietnam. This has been felt most keenly by those Americans and Canadians who have been sponsors of Vietnamese refugees and have come to know them well on a daily basis. The settlement of a refugee family in rural Coldwater, Ontario (population 1,000), "really broadened our horizons," said one resident. "In a place like this, contact with other races is not something that happens every day."

Living with Vietnamese in their midst has been a lesson in compassion and tolerance for North Americans. The United States had always been proud of being a welcoming refuge for the needy and a melting pot where many cultures could blend together; Canada had an official policy of encouraging ethnic diversity and the preservation of distinct cultures. Yet some people of both countries were overwhelmed with the large numbers of refugees and feared them as an economic threat. Studies have shown that, like other immigrants, Vietnamese often take jobs that others do not want, and more than make up for their government aid by paying taxes and making investments.

Still, there are incidents of intolerance toward Vietnamese. In the late 1970's, the Ku Klux Klan harassed Vietnamese fishermen on the Gulf Coast. In the early 1980's, unproven rumors spread about Vietnamese eating household pets and contaminating food on grocery shelves in the town of Stockton, California. (In fact, some villagers in Vietnam do eat dog meat, but this is extremely rare in America.) In 1989, a gunman fired an automatic rifle into a schoolyard in Stockton, killing five Vietnamese and Cambodian children and wounding twenty-nine others; he was later found to have long resented Southeast Asian refugees being resettled in America. The same

A new generation of Americans enjoy the Tet festival as celebrated in Southern California. Completely immersed in American society, these youngsters keep important aspects of their heritage and culture alive.

year, 62 percent of Vietnamese surveyed in Orange County said they felt there was "a lot" or "some" prejudice against Vietnamese in the United States, though most had not felt the effects of it themselves.

FROM REFUGEES TO CITIZENS

Perhaps this situation will change with time as the Vietnamese are more integrated into American communities and as Asian Americans become more powerful in American life. After all, it is Vietnamese refugees and immigrants who are largely responsible for the phenomenal growth in the Asian-Pacific population from 1980 to 1990. They are also singled out as a particularly remarkable "model minority" among Asians for their rapid rise to success. As the third largest Asian-Pacific group in the United States, the Vietnamese are bound to play an increasingly important role in this community. For example, one Vietnamese candidate is currently running for election to the Board of Supervisors in heavily Asian-American San Francisco.

The Vietnamese are still coming of age as a part of American society. More than 143,000 of them became U.S. citizens between 1979 and 1988. They are making the shift from reluctant refugees to Vietnamese Americans with the same rights and responsibilities as other Americans. This is an indication of the contributions they will continue to make to American life in years to come.

FAMOUS

VIETNAMESE AMERICANS

Many Vietnamese have distinguished themselves during their short years in America. The 1989 *Who's Who in California*, for instance, lists dozens of notable Vietnamese doctors, lawyers, engineers, chemists, educators, businessmen, and other professionals. However, since little information is available in English on nationally famous Vietnamese, those described below are only a small sample, compiled from the American media and Vietnamese community organizations.

POLITICS

Some famous politicians from Vietnam remain well-known in America. Nguyen Cao Ky, an air force pilot war hero who became premier of South Vietnam in the 1960's, originally settled in a mansion in Alexandria, Virginia, and toured the 1975 refugee camps, hoping to reestablish his leadership; he later moved to Orange County, California, and became a businessman. Nguyen Huy Ngoc, who was part of the South Vietnamese delegation to the Paris peace talks in 1968-1970, lives in Cambridge, Massachusetts, where he has taught Vietnamese history and politics at Harvard University.

EDUCATION

Academic honors have been received by many Vietnamese. By age twenty-six, Tue Nguyen, once a boat person, had received seven advanced degrees from the Massachusetts

Institute of Technology (MIT), including a Ph.D. in nuclear
engineering. Kien Pham, a graduate of Stanford Business
School, was one of fourteen White House Fellowship
awardees in 1985-1986; he was particularly proud of the
volunteer work he did in refugee camps in Asia. Hoang Nhu
Tran, who came to the United States in 1975 at age nine,
graduated from the U.S. Air Force Academy with top honors
in 1987 and want on to become one of thirty-two American
winners of a prestigious Rhodes scholarship to Oxford
University. "My parents always impressed upon me that when
you receive a gift from the nation, as I have, you should
always give something back," he said of his plans to become
a doctor.

Other Vietnamese are the first of their people to make their
mark in prestigious fields. Dr. Eugene Trinh became an
astronaut with NASA after earning a Ph.D. in physics at Yale.
Jean Nguyen and Hung Vu, both from South Vietnamese
military families, became the first Vietnamese graduates of the
U.S. Military Academy at West Point in 1985.

ARTS, ENTERTAINMENT, AND SPORTS

A number of Vietnamese are active in writing, translating,
and promoting Vietnamese literature. A five-year MacArthur
Fellowship, often called the "genius award," was given to Dr.
Huynh Sanh Thong of Yale University in 1987 for his work in
bringing Vietnamese classics to English-speaking readers. Vo
Thien of Southern California is beloved by Vietnamese for his
sad stories; novelist Nguyen Ngan Ngoc writes about
Vietnamese life in both Vietnam and Canada and is president
of the Vietnamese PEN writers' organization.

In arts and entertainment, numerous Vietnamese pop singers
entertain the community at Tet celebrations, variety shows, and
through cassettes and videos. One of the best known poet-
composers is Pham Duy, who performed at the American

Vietnamese-born American actor Dustin Nguyen.

refugee camps in 1975. His songs urge Vietnamese to keep their traditions and the hope of someday returning to Vietnam. Visual artists include Vo Dinh, whose paintings and woodcut prints can be seen in galleries in Washington, D.C., and painter-sculptor Nguyen Trung The, recently arrived in Toronto, whose works have been reproduced on postcards to raise funds for United Nations programs. A handful of Vietnamese actors have appeared in American film and television, most notably Dustin Nguyen of "21 Jump Street." The son of a television producer in Vietnam, he grew up a loner in St. Louis and got into acting by accident in college; he now lives in Vancouver, Canada.

There are as yet few famous Vietnamese athletes. One exception is Mike Nguyen, who was only two when he left Vietnam. He received a sports scholarship to UCLA and is the first Vietnamese to play major college football. A hard worker who holds down two part-time jobs and a high grade-point average, he says he was raised to "be an asset to [my] family and [my] community."

COMMUNITY SERVICE

Many Vietnamese are famous for the dedicated service they have given to community organizations. Some come to this work from other professions, such as Le Xuan Khoa, formerly a philosophy professor and a vice president of Saigon University. Since 1983, he has directed the Indochina Resource Action Center in Washington, D.C., which works to defend refugee rights and strengthen Southeast Asian communities in the United States.

Vietnamese-Canadian psychiatrist Dr. Nguyen San Buy has headed a number of medical teams that reported on conditions at Asian refugee camps. Dr. Can Le was recently honored by the Ontario government for his efforts as head of the Vietnamese Refugee Sponsorship Coordinating Council of

Canada, which helps set up private sponsors for refugees still in Asian camps.

RELIGION

Among well-known Vietnamese religious leaders was the late Ven. Thich Thien-An, who died in 1980. He was a Buddhist monk and scholar who came to the United States in 1966 to teach language and philosophy at UCLA. He founded the International Buddhist Meditation Center in Los Angeles in 1970 and later the Vietnamese Buddhist Temple, eventually becoming Supreme Abbot for Vietnamese Buddhists in North America. He is the author of three important books on Zen Buddhism.

ACHIEVEMENTS BY VIETNAMESE WOMEN

Vietnamese women are increasingly making their mark as accomplished individuals. They include Vu Thanh Thuy, a former war correspondent in Vietnam, coauthor of *Pirates in the Gulf of Siam* and other accounts of the boat people's experience. In 1987 she received the $20,000 21st Century Woman Award from the National Organization for Women. Le Ly Hayslip has won praise for her 1989 autobiography, *When Heaven and Earth Changed Places: A Vietnamese Woman's Journey from War to Peace*, soon to be made into a movie. It tells the story of how she came of age during the Vietnam War working for the Viet Cong, enduring prison, torture, rape, and hunger before leaving for the United States with her American husband in 1970. It also describes her reunion with her family in Vietnam in 1986, and the work of the East Meets West Foundation which Hayslip founded to fund health clinics in Vietnam.

The stories of these famous Vietnamese contain some of the same contrasts and challenges that have marked the lives of all Vietnamese Americans. No doubt the longer they live in

America, the better known the Vietnamese will become to other Americans—both as impressive individuals and as a remarkable people who have made a unique journey from their homeland to a new land.

AMERICAN VOICES

VIETNAMESE AMERICANS

TIME LINE

208– 111 B.C.	The indigenous kingdom of Nam Viet flourishes.
111 B.C.– A.D. 939	Vietnam endures 1,000 years of Chinese rule.
939– 1883	Vietnam enjoys 900 years of independence under various local dynasties.
1883– 1945	French colonialists rule in Vietnam.
1945	Ho Chi Minh declares the independent Democratic Republic of Vietnam.
1946– 1954	First Indochina War breaks out between France and the Viet Minh.
1954	The Geneva Accords divide the country into North and South Vietnam.
1955– 1975	Second Indochina War, called the Vietnam War, pits North Vietnam against the coalition troops of South Vietnam and the United States.
1973	The Paris Peace treaty is signed and American troops leave Vietnam.
1975	On April 30 ("Day of Anguish"), Saigon, the capital of South Vietnam, falls to Communist troops, marking the end of the Vietnam War; 65,000 South Vietnamese are evacuated by U.S. government.
1975	Four American camps receive 125,000 refugees and match them up with sponsors; the first wave of Vietnamese immigrants. The Indochina Migration and Refugee Assistance Act gives $405 million to resettle refugees in the United States.

1976-	More refugees are admitted under special paroles.
1977	Secondary migration of first-wave refugees to form communities in larger American cities begins.
	Chua Viet Nam is founded in Los Angeles, the first Vietnamese Buddhist temple in the United States.
1978	Chinese Vietnamese flee overland to China and by boat to Southeast Asian ports in response to persecution; beginning of the boat people exodus.
	Vietnam invades neighboring Cambodia.
1979	Border war between Vietnam and China erupts. Boat people continue to leave in large numbers, suffer hardships and piracy on ships, are refused rescue and refuge.
	The Geneva Conference on Indochinese Refugees is convened by United Nations to find solutions to the boat people crisis.
	The Indochinese Refugee Assistance Program gives cash payments to support refugees for up to three years after arriving in the United States.
	Tensions between Vietnamese and Mexican Americans over housing (riot at Denver housing project) and between Vietnamese and American fishermen (murder of American by Vietnamese in Seadrift, Texas; harassment of Vietnamese fishermen by the Ku Klux Klan).
1979-	United States and Canada admit increased numbers of boat
1981	people; the second wave of Vietnamese immigrants.
1980	The Refugee Act of 1980 redefines the term "refugee" according to United Nations standards; United States allows large-scale admissions of Cambodians fleeing mass killings in their homeland. U.S. census counts 245,000 Vietnamese: one-third live in poverty but one-fourth own their own homes.
1981	U.S. government funding of refugee assistance programs peaks at $902 million.
1982	Vietnamese refugee admissions decline dramatically in United States and Canada and stay that way for next eight years; the third wave of Vietnamese immigrants.
	Thousands of boat people are still held in camps in Southeast Asia with no place to go.

1983	The Orderly Departure Program begins allowing legal immigration of Vietnamese to be reunited with relatives in the United States.
	The Refugee Act of 1983 limits welfare benefits for refugees to the first eighteen months after arrival in the United States.
1985	The incomes of first-wave Vietnamese Americans reach the U.S. average.
	A tenth-year reunion at Camp Pendleton attracts 30,000 first-wave Vietnamese.
1986	Canadian census counts 63,000 Vietnamese residing in Canadian provinces.
1987	The Amerasian Homecoming Act allows for legal immigration of Amerasian teenagers and their families with refugee benefits.
1988	Southeast Asian countries of first asylum begin closing their doors to boat people with screening process that denies them refugee status and assistance.
1989	Stockton, California, schoolyard massacre leaves five Indochinese children dead.
	U.S. government cash assistance to refugees reduced to one year after arrival.
	Vietnamese troops withdraw from Cambodia.
1990	A suit by the Vietnamese Fishermen's Association wins right of noncitizens to own and operate commercial fishing boats off the California coast.
	100,000 Vietnamese boat people remain in camps in Southeast Asia, the highest total since 1979.
	First group of 150 former South Vietnamese political prisoners immigrate to United States under a new program.
1991	Early U.S. census figures show Vietnamese are third largest Asian-American group.

GLOSSARY

Amerasians: Children born to Asian and American parents. Specifically in this book, the term refers to children born in Vietnam during the Vietnam War to Vietnamese mothers and American fathers.

Ancestor worship: The tradition of showing respect for ancestors of the past five generations through special prayers and ceremonies on anniversaries of their deaths and holidays.

Boat people: Vietnamese refugees (often of ethnic Chinese origin) who left or escaped Vietnam by boat after 1978.

Buddhism: The main religion of Vietnam which originated in India in fifth century B.C.; its beliefs include the search for enlightenment through meditation and virtue, the concept of past lives determining the present, and the quest for detachment from the material world.

Communism: A political and economic system which favors the holding of all property in common by the state rather than privately; may involve one-party rule by Communist Party.

Confucianism: An ethical system brought to Vietnam by Chinese; beliefs include ancestor worship, filial piety (obedience to parents), the appointment of rulers based on education and merit, and submission to the authority of just rulers.

Countries of first asylum: Countries where Vietnamese refugees sought temporary refuge while awaiting final settlement (Hong Kong, Indonesia, Malaysia, Philippines, and Thailand).

Ethnic Chinese: A minority of Chinese origin, also called Chinese Vietnamese or Hoa, who were prominent in trade and business, with their own language, customs, and neighborhoods in Vietnam.

Extended family: A household consisting of at least three generations (children, parents, grandparents); common in traditional Vietnamese families.

First-wave refugees: Vietnamese immigrants who came to America in 1975-1978 after the end of the Vietnam War.

Guerrilla war: A method of combat consisting of surprise attacks and ambushes on many fronts rather than large, conventional battles on one or few fronts.

Immigrants: People who make plans to leave their country for permanent settlement elsewhere to pursue better opportunities (compare with *refugees*).

Indochinese: Peoples of Vietnam, Kampuchea (formerly Cambodia), and Laos on the Indochina peninsula in Southeast Asia, many of whom came to the United States as refugees after 1975.

Mandarin: Under Chinese rule, Vietnamese and Chinese government officials who were appointed based on their education and merit.

Nationalism: The belief that the people living in a country (rather than outside forces) have a right to determine their own future as an independent nation.

Parole: A method of bypassing the usual rules for screening immigrants, used to admit Vietnamese refugees to United States before 1980 by special decree of the Attorney General.

Reeducation camps: Places in Vietnam where certain South Vietnamese were sent against their will after 1975 to work camps and were forcibly taught Communist beliefs.

Refugees: People who flee their country in haste or are forced to leave due to fear of persecution and seek a safe haven (often temporary) elsewhere; in the United States, they are eligible for special government benefits (compare with *immigrants*).

Second-wave refugees: Vietnamese immigrants who came to the United States from 1978 to 1982 as part of the peak years of the boat people crisis.

Secondary migration: The movement of refugees or immigrants from their original place of settlement to a second location within their adopted country.

Sponsor: A family, individual, organization, company, or committee that takes financial and moral responsibility for helping a refugee household get settled in the United States or Canada.

Tet: Vietnamese New Year celebrated in late January or early February.

Third wave: The reduced numbers of Vietnamese refugees and immigrants who have come to the U.S. and Canada since 1982.

Viet Cong: South Vietnamese who fought on the side of the Communist North Vietnamese during the Vietnam War.

VOLAG: A private voluntary agency that works with the U.S. government to coordinate refugee sponsorship and resettlement.

89

RESOURCES

Center for Applied Linguistics
3520 Prospect St., N.W.
Washington, D.C. 20007
(202) 298-9292
    The center provides research and educational materials about and for
Indochinese refugees and their sponsors in English and Vietnamese.

Indochina Resource Action Center (IRAC)
1628 16th St., N.W.
Washington, D.C. 20009
(202) 667-4690
    IRAC offers for information on Indochinese refugees, public education
and advocacy for refugee rights and protection, and technical assistance
and empowerment to refugee community. The center also publishes a
newsletter, *The Bridge*.

Interaction Amerasian Resettlement Program
200 Park Ave., South, Suite 1115
New York, NY 10003
(212) 777-8210
    Information about, advocacy for, and refugee resettlement assistance to
Amerasian youth (children of Asian mothers and American fathers) and
their families is provided by this agency.

International Rescue Committee
386 Park Ave. S.
New York, NY 10016
(212) 679-0010
    One of the two largest private voluntary agencies (VOLAGs) involved
in sponsorship of and service to Vietnamese refugees since 1975.

Office of Refugee Resettlement (ORR)
Dept. of Health and Human Services
Switzer Bldg., Rm. 1229
330 "C" St., S.W.
Washington, D.C. 20201
(202) 401-4548
   ORR funds and coordinates social services, English instruction, vocational training, medical assistance and other refugee programs throughout the United States; compiles refugee statistics; and prepares an annual report to Congress.

Research Resource Division for Refugees
Centre for Immigration and Ethno-Cultural Studies, Room 112A
Carlton University
Social Science Research Bldg.
Ottawa, Ontario K1S 5B6
Canada
   This Canadian organization provides research assistance and publishes the newsletter *INSCAN* about Indochinese refugees in Canada.

U.S. Catholic Conference, Migration and Refugee Services
3211 4th St., N.E.
Washington, D.C. 20017
(202) 541-3000
   Along with the International Rescue Committee, this agency is one of the largest private voluntary agencies (VOLAGs) involved in sponsorship of and service to Vietnamese refugees.

U.S. Coordinator for Refugee Affairs
Dept. of State
Washington, D.C. 20520
(202) 632-5430
   This office coordinates various federal agencies involved in refugee policy and programs.

Vietnamese Buddhist Center
863 S. Berendo
Los Angeles, CA 90025
(213) 384-9638

The center maintains the oldest Vietnamese Buddhist temple in the United States with religious and community activities in both Vietnamese and English; publishes some booklets on Buddhism.

Vietnamese Canadian Federation
249 Rochester St.
Ottawa, Ontario K1R 7M9
Canada
The federation coordinates the activities of nineteen provincial and city Vietnamese associations across Canada; sponsors resource center/library with information on Vietnamese and Vietnamese-Canadian history, culture, and other topics relating to the Vietnamese experience in Canada.

Vietnamese Chamber of Commerce in America
9872 Chapman Ave., Suite 9A
Garden Grove, CA 92641
(714) 530-2733
This trade organization provides publications and workshops in Vietnamese on business management and publishes Vietnamese business directories.

Vietnamese Community of Orange County, Inc.
3701 McFadden Ave., Suites M-N
Santa Ana, CA 92704
(714) 775-2637
A mutual assistance agency for the largest Vietnamese community in the United States with elderly and youth services, job training, English classes, information and referral, and other social services.

BIBLIOGRAPHY

Day, Carol Olsen and Edmund Day. *The New Immigrants*. New York: Franklin Watts/Impact Books, 1985. Aimed at readers from grades six through twelve, this is a general account of changes in U.S. immigration law and the new Asian and Latino immigrants of the last twenty years, with sections on Vietnamese refugees.

Fields, Rick, with photography by Don Farber. *Taking Refuge in L.A.: Life in a Vietnamese Buddhist Temple*. New York: Aperture Foundation, 1987. Excellent photographic study of daily life in a Vietnamese-American temple. Text traces history of Vietnamese Buddhism and Buddhist customs in the United States.

Freeman, James M. *Hearts of Sorrow: Vietnamese-American Lives*. Stanford, Calif.: Stanford University Press, 1989. Life stories as told by fourteen Vietnamese Americans, between the ages sixteen and eighty, ranging from auto mechanics to Buddhist nuns. Covers their early experience in Vietnam, the war years, flight to the United States, and settlement in San Jose area. The most recent and complete study to date of Vietnamese Americans.

Haskins, James. *The New Americans: Vietnamese Boat People*. Hillside, N.J.: Enslow Publishers, 1980. A general account for young people of the story of the boat people with many dramatic photos.

Kelly, Gail Paradise. *From Vietnam to America: A Chronicle of the Vietnamese Immigration to the United States*. Boulder, Colo.: Westview Press, 1977. The first important study of first-wave Vietnamese Americans. Stresses their flight from Vietnam in 1975 and experience in American refugee camps, with survey information on who these people were (age, sex, family size, job, religion, and so forth).

Knoll, Tricia. *Becoming Americans: Asian Sojourners, Immigrants and Refugees in the Western United States*. Portland, Ore.: Coast to Coast Books, 1982. Lively chapters on first-wave Vietnamese refugees and Chinese-Vietnamese boat people put in the context of Asian-American immigration history. Includes many personal stories, photos, and helpful maps.

Rutledge, Paul. *The Vietnamese in America.* Minneapolis, Minn.: Lerner Publications, 1987. Part of the "In America" Series, this book is an easy-to-read, illustrated survey of Vietnamese immigration to the United States and the adjustment and contribution of Vietnamese immigrants to American life, especially in the Midwest.

Sheldon, Walter J. *Tigers in the Rice: The Story of Vietnam from Ancient Past to Uncertain Future.* New York: Macmillan, 1969. Clear, concise history of Vietnam stressing nineteenth and twentieth century events up to the beginning of the Paris peace talks, written for middle school and high school students.

Stanek, Muriel. *We Came from Vietnam.* Niles, Ill.: Albert Whitman, 1985. Portrait of Nguyen family from their native village in Vietnam to daily life in Chicago including family activities, holidays, shopping, school, and other experiences. An easy-to-read juvenile book with photos.

Thuy, Vuong G. *Getting to Know the Vietnamese and Their Culture.* New York: Frederick Ungar, 1976. Useful introduction to Vietnamese cultural and social customs, though sometimes makes generalizations which are no longer true for Vietnamese life in the United States.

Warren, James A. *Portrait of a Tragedy: America and the Vietnam War.* New York: Lothrup, Lee and Shepard, 1990. For juvenile readers, this survey provides a complete illustrated history of the United States' twenty-five-year involvement in the Vietnam War and its effect on American society.

Wright, David K. *Vietnam.* Chicago: Children's Press, 1989. Part of "Enchantment of the World" series for young readers, this book provides an overview of Vietnamese history and modern life since 1975 by an authority on the Vietnam War. Excellent color photographs, time lines, and "mini-facts at a glance."

Wright, Mary Bowen. "Indochinese." In *Harvard Encyclopedia of American Ethnic Groups.* Edited by Stephan Thernstrom. Cambridge, Mass.: The Belknap Press of Harvard University Press, 1980. Summary of the ethnic background and immigration experience of first wave Vietnamese and other Indochinese refugees.

MEDIA BIBLIOGRAPHY

DOCUMENTARY FILMS

Fire on the Water. Directed by Robert Hillman. 56 minutes, 16mm, 1982. Available from Cinergy Films, Robert Hillman Associates, 2600 10th St., Berkeley, CA 94710. Documents prejudice against Vietnamese on Texas Gulf Coast by focusing on a young Vietnamese fisherman and his family, an American boat mechanic from the Ku Klux Klan, and others. Received Blue Ribbon award at American Film festival.

Overture: Linh from Vietnam. 26 minutes, 16mm, 1981. Available from Learning Corp. of America, Simon & Schuster, 108 Wilmost Road, Deerfield, IL 60015. Focuses on young refugee Linh Tran and her family's adjustment to American life, showing the conflicts and common interest between Vietnamese and Mexican students.

The Story of Vinh. Directed by Keiko Tsuno. 58 minutes, videocassette, 1990. For information, contact Crosscurrent Media, National Asian American Telecommunications Association, 346 9th St., San Francisco, CA 94103. Traces life of a sixteen-year-old Amerasian boy from his life on the streets in Vietnam to foster homes and a difficult adjustment in America.

Thanh's War. Produced by Elizabeth Farnsworth. 58 minutes, videocassette, 1990. For information, contact KQED-TV, 500 8th St., San Francisco, CA 94103. Story of a twelve-year-old Vietnamese boy critically injured in the war who reluctantly came to the United States for surgery and eventually became a proud but divided Vietnamese American. Fascinating footage of his emotional return visits to Vietnam as an adult and his wedding to a woman from his native village.

Vietnam Perspective. 32 minutes, 16mm or videocassette, 1985. Available from Encyclopedia Brittanica Educational Corporation, 425 N. Michigan Ave., Chicago, IL 60611. Describes foreign involvement in Southeast Asia with stress on the American role in Vietnam War.

Vietnamese Buddhism in America and *Vietnamese Refugees in America.* 14 minutes each, videocassette, n.d. Part of series *Asians in America.*

95

Available from Centre Productions, 1800 30th St., Suite #207, Boulder, CO 80301. Two brief films on Vietnamese Buddhist leader Dr. Thich Thien-An and on the general problems and achievements of Vietnamese refugees in the United States.

Way of the Willow. 30 minutes, 16mm, 1982. Available from Beacon Films, P.O. Box 575, Norwood, MA 02062. Describes challenges faced by a family of Vietnamese boat people who settle in a Canadian city.

MUSIC

From Rice Paddies and Temple Yards: Traditional Music of Vietnam. Cassette tape and book produced by Phong Nguyen and Patricia Campbell. Available from World Music Press, P.O. Box 2565, Danbury, CT 06813. An introduction to various styles and regions of the music of Vietnam, designed for students.

TELEVISION PROGRAMS

Down Home (1990-present). On this series, a Vietnamese immigrant is employed as a cook in a small-town diner located on Texas' Gulf Coast. Although a Japanese-American actor portrays this character, the show does reflect the growth of a Vietnamese-American community in this part of Texas.

Night Court (1984-present). One of the recurring roles on this situation comedy set in a New York City criminal night court is the Vietnamese wife of the court clerk, Mac Robinson, a black Vietnam veteran. Although the show relies on stereotypes and broad humor for its comedy, its depiction of an interracial marriage is admirable.

St. Elsewhere (1982-1986). Veteran actress France Nuyen joined the cast in the final years as Dr. Paulette Kiem, a Vietnamese-American surgeon appointed to the staff of St. Eligius, a Boston-area teaching hospital.

Together We Stand/Nothing Is Easy (1987-1987). Ke Huy Quan, the young actor from the second Indiana Jones film, was featured as Sam Randall, the teenage Asian son adopted by a suburban American family headed by Elliot Gould.

21 Jump Street (1987-1989). Vietnamese-American actor Dustin Nguyen played Harry Truman "H.T." Ioki, an Asian-American undercover policeman who, along with three other young cops, infiltrated Los Angeles area high schools to combat drug dealers and teen gangs.

NOVELS

Dunn, Mary Lois. *The Man in the Box: A Story from Vietnam.* New York: McGraw-Hill, 1968. A Montagnard boy from a Vietnamese hill tribe saves the life of an American soldier who is imprisoned in a box. Reveals Montagnard customs and the horrors of the Vietnam War while describing the friendship between the boy and the soldier.

Gilson, Jamie. *Hello, My Name is Scrambled Eggs.* New York: Lothrop, Lee and Shepard Books, 1985. The adventures, jokes, lessons, and friendships that result when an Illinois family sponsors five Vietnamese refugees, with a focus on twelve-year-olds Harvey Trumble and Tuan Nguyen.

Wartski, Maureen Crane. *A Long Way From Home.* Philadephia: Westminister Press, 1980. The story of a fifteen-year-old Vietnamese refugee who has trouble "belonging" in American culture and runs away to a Vietnamese fishing community.

AMERICAN VOICES

VIETNAMESE AMERICANS

INDEX

DUE DATE